W9-DDM-941

THE
DRESDEN GALLERY

THE DRESDEN GALLERY

HENNER MENZ

LONDON
THAMES AND HUDSON

TRANSLATED FROM THE GERMAN
BY DAPHNE WOODWARD

THIS EDITION © THAMES AND HUDSON LONDON 1962
© EDITION AIMERY SOMOGY PARIS 1962
PRINTED BY CARL SCHÜNEMANN GERMANY

CONTENTS

KUNSTKAMMER

Any attempt to retrace the history of the Dresden Art Gallery to its first inception must ultimately lead back to one of those collections of *objets d'art* and curiosities which were a characteristic feature of German royal households in the late sixteenth and seventeenth century.

These 'cabinets' served as a repository for every kind of supposedly or genuinely valuable object that appealed to the human fancy – from works of art, freakish, rare or ludicrous exhibits, souvenirs, gifts, religious articles, books and *topographica*, to natural history specimens and technical appliances.

As late as 1727, by which time such accumulations had gone out of fashion, Caspar F. Neickel, a Hamburg merchant with a lively interest in the subject of collections, included in his *Museographia* (published by Michael Hubert at Leipzig and Breslau) some suggestions for the arrangement of 'cabinets' of this kind. Being concise and deliberately simplified, they give a clear idea of what the general effect must have been.

Neickel recommends that to avert the ever-present danger of untidiness, the room used shall be well lit and uncluttered 'so that even the smallest of its contents may be visible'. The actual collections should be 'protected from any mishap' in specially constructed 'Repositoriis' (in cupboards and on shelves).

The *Museographia* insists that definite principles shall govern the arrangement. There are to be two prime categories, 'Naturalia' and 'Curiosa Artificialia', within which 'a principal division between antique and modern is in particular to be made, but with such manner of arrangement that both the artistic quality and the purpose of the objects may be discerned'. To facilitate this, there should be a convenient table in the middle of the room, 'upon which rarities brought forth for contemplation may be laid out and examined, or sundry books, if asked for, may be consulted and read over'.

7

Pictures – the main subject of interest to the historian of an art gallery – are not touched on by Neickel until the end of his description, where he remarks casually that 'Any space remaining above the windows and Repositoriis may be filled up with rare paintings by famous Masters.'

The author of the *Museographia* is merely an uncritical copyist of long out-dated source material; but the historian will find the book instructive because on the one hand it is still concerned with the characteristic features of the old 'cabinets' of works of art and curiosities, while on the other it already indicates the course of future developments.

At the beginning of his enumeration of an enormous variety of items, Neickel puts a *Theatrum Mundi* which, in its claim to be all-embracing, goes far to satisfy the medieval concept of the *Summae* and thus gives purpose to the whole idea of the passionate collector. Quantity is emphasized throughout as the decisive factor.

The ancient notion of the 'treasure-house' comes into it too. It is to be an assemblage of 'valuable' things. And value was less a matter of aesthetic quality, as it is nowadays, than of costly materials – noble metals and precious stones, – rarity and oddity, so that the word 'art' should rather be understood in the sense of 'artifice'. It must be remembered that the hoarding of treasures is an expression of the primitive will to power, and the pompous displays by which rulers evidenced their might should not be underestimated in any account of the origin of art collections. Consequently, Neickel practically ignores the aesthetic appeal of valuable objects, which is an aspect which fascinates a modern collector. Even pictures are not appreciated for their quality, but for possessing 'rarity value'.

It should not be forgotten, however, that in those days collections in the present-day sense of the word had already existed for a long time, on a level far above that of the ordinary 'cabinet of curiosities'.

In Italy, for instance, the memory of classical times, with their art collections, had been preserved through the centuries much more vividly than in the North; and as early as the fifteenth century Italy had important specialized collections which could not have come

8

into existence without a strong feeling for art. And though such a man as Jean de France, Duc de Berry (1340–1416), with his enthusiasm for collecting fine works of art and his rejection of all others, was still an exceptional figure in Northern Europe, his collector's zeal provides an early example of the manner in which aesthetic appreciation can outweigh all other motives. Rudolf II of Habsburg (1522–1612) also belonged entirely to the new age, for he was not solely concerned with completeness, in the sense of the ancient *Theatrum Mundi*, nor with the piling up of the objects of intrinsic value; he enjoyed the fact of owning works of art that appealed to his personal taste. It is touching as well as significant to remember that on the arrival of a statue by Giovanni da Bologna which he had been eagerly awaiting, he clasped it in his arms, crying 'Now this is mine!' –after which it disappeared at once into his private cabinet, where he could feast his eyes on it whenever he chose. Even so, his art gallery in the Hradčany at Prague bore little resemblance to a present-day museum. In its system of storage and display it was more like the other 'cabinets of curiosities' described in contemporary reports. Efforts were already being made to introduce the kind of orderliness that Neickel had in mind; but we still find frequent complaints of cramped accommodation, packed coffers and boxes, confusion and total lack of method.

The idea of specialization was already implied in Neickel's advocacy of systematic arrangement, which could be arrived at only by dividing a collection into sections; and museums were, indeed, to develop in that direction.

This was facilitated by the realization that an art gallery should not be primarily a storehouse, treasury, hobby-room or workshop for its princely owner, but a place for contemplation or even for research, where the visitor could sit comfortably at a table and examine the different pieces in the collection, with the appropriate reference books at hand to provide him with fuller information. This idea reveals Neickel as a true product of the eighteenth century, which developed such a passion for Academies.

The sixteenth century had not nearly reached this point, of course,

9

though one ruler, at any rate—Duke Albrecht V of Bavaria (1528–1579)—went so far as to divide his collection into sections, according to subject. He was a versatile aesthete and music-lover who sent for the ingenious Orlando di Lasso to be his Court composer, and he had an 'Antiquarium' built next to his *Kunstkammer* to house his extensive collection of antiques. There was no trace of this spirit in Augustus I, Elector of Saxony (1526–1586), who had a *Kunstkammer* arranged in his palace at Dresden in the year 1560. He was a practical-minded ruler, bearing no resemblance either to Rudolf II, with his flamboyant enthusiasm for art, or to Albrecht of Bavaria, with his surprisingly 'modern' ideas about museum arrangement. In contrast to his princely neighbours—judicious art collectors but political weaklings,—he was a thorough realist, circumspect, vigorous to the point of brutality, and firmly resolved on extending and consolidating his power. The Muses played little part in shaping his character. As the owner of the largest domains, he succeeded in developing the country's economy in a manner which provided him with ample means of furthering his expansionist policy and displaying his splendour. The Freiberg silver-mines were flourishing. The profits from them flowed straight into the princely coffers and counterbalanced the expenditure required to eliminate competition.

Augustus I successfully tackled such problems as the reorganization of the government, the drafting of a unified code of laws, the support of the Leipzig Fair, systematic land surveying, and the introduction of a permanent messenger and mail service. In 1574 he became an orthodox Lutheran and thereafter relentlessly persecuted the Calvinists, whose bourgeois tendencies he regarded—quite rightly, as the history of the Wars of Independence in the Netherlands was to show—as a danger to feudalism and consequently to his own power. Thus it came about that his art collection, in its wealth and variety, was intended first and foremost as an imposing manifestation of the brilliance and power of a ruler, who necessarily attached great importance to constantly adding to it by fresh purchases. Many fine pieces came to Dresden as gifts, too, for once a collection of treasures has been formed it acts as a magnet for other valuable objects. Parti-

10

culars of how the collection was built up and what it comprised are given in an inventory prepared in 1587, a year after the death of Augustus I, on the instructions of his son and successor, Christian I (1560–1591). The art gallery was made up of seven rooms, situated immediately above the Elector's own apartments. Only five of these rooms were fitted up, the two others – small ones next door to which was a turner's workshop where Augustus himself had sometimes put his hand to the lathe – being used as reserve and lumber-rooms.

The palace at Dresden, first mentioned in the records in 1285, had been repeatedly enlarged since 1382. During the period between 1530 and 1556, thanks to the work of two architects, Hans Dehn-Roth-felser and Caspar Voigt von Wierlandt, it grew to be one of the most impressive and important examples of renaissance architecture in Germany, with its spacious courtyard, its magnificent carved gates and the loggia below its main tower. As the residence of the Elector of Saxony, the palace was no less splendid than the *Kunstkammer* within its walls.

The inventory lists the items of the collection room by room, revealing at least some attempt to arrange them according to subject. The largest category comprises measuring instruments, scientific apparatus, globes and maps, craftsmen's tools, clocks and automata, testifying to the prosaic and practical tastes of the ruler, who was particularly interested in geography and surveying.

Apart from the works of classical writers the 288 volumes in the library, too, constisted chiefly of books on mathematics, technology, geography and astronomy. Theological, medical and legal books were kept in another place.

Prominent among the natural history items was a valuable collection of geological specimens. But there was also an example of the legendary unicorn's horn, suspended from the ceiling by a golden chain. Many descriptions mention this tusk as a rare and precious item in the collection.

In comparison with the vast number of fine examples of craftsmanship – goldsmith's work, ivory pieces (some of which had been partly turned by the Elector himself), coins, bronze statues, furniture

11

and musical instruments–actual works of art form a very small proportion of the contents. This was in contrast to the collections made by Albrecht of Bavaria and Rudolf II, or that of the Archduke Ferdinand in his castle at Ambras in the Tyrol. There is a striking dearth of antiques, which were such an outstanding feature of the *Kunstkammer* at Munich. A visitor looking for pictures would find without difficulty those which flattered the dynastic sense of a prince with a taste for display. Every art gallery had its collection of portraits of the ruling house, which it was sometimes found possible, by straining probability a little, to carry back as far as the Roman Emperors.

Pictures of hunting trophies were also very popular. Paintings of particularly fine beasts or birds, and portraits of favourite dogs, were kept as souvenirs. These and their like were hung in no special order on any empty spaces on the walls of the Dresden Gallery, as Neickel noted in his *Museographia* 140 years later.

It is difficult to identify the individual paintings in retrospect, for most of them have disappeared and the inventory descriptions are often incomplete and inaccurate. Moreover, incorrect entries were apt to be copied from one catalogue into the next, and were often not rectified for years, if at all.

The only important artists mentioned in the 1587 inventory are Hans Bol and Lucas Cranach the Elder. Cranach had been Court painter to the Elector of Saxony at Wittenberg on the Elbe from 1505 onwards, and had left a considerable body of work at his death. This makes it all the more surprising that at this time the collection contained only two pictures by him–*Adam* and *Eve*, painted in 1531 (Gal. nos. 1911 and 1912). These are still preserved. The present contents of the Gallery also include five of the original sixteen pictures by Hans Bol, the Dutch landscape painter and miniaturist, which are praised as 'pretty little paintings'. These are *Water Tournament on the Vijver at The Hague* (Gal. no. 822), *Village Fair* (Gal. no. 823), *Jacob's Dream* (Gal. no. 828), *Meleager and Atalanta* (Gal. no. 829), and *Moses and the Daughters of Jethro at the Well* (Gal. no. 830). Four others were acquired later.

12

The *Village Fair* and the *Meleager* picture are dated 1580 and the *Tournament* 1586, so these small water-colours were contemporary works, bought as soon as they were painted. Pictures destroyed in the second World War included two portraits, of the Elector Augustus of Saxony and of his consort, Anne, painted by Hans Krell, who worked at Leipzig and Freiberg and died in the former town about the year 1586.

This modest group of pictures gives no hint of the famous art gallery which, in course of time, was to form round such a small nucleus.

The inventories subsequent to 1587 show great numbers of new acquisitions of all kinds, particularly after 1601, when Christian II (1583–1611) came to the throne. Very few of these have been preserved. Signs of an increase in the number of pictures admitted are very evident, however. As well as the usual portraits of the ruling family, known in the inventories as *Contrafecten*, biblical and mythological subjects begin to appear. The entry for September 1588 mentions that 'two canvases painted in oils, one showing the *Triumph of Bacchus* and the other *Judith and Holophernes*, have been made by Bartholomaeus Spranger, painter to His Imperial Majesty.'

It is a great pity that these particular works have disappeared, for as examples of Spranger's painting they would have made a most valuable addition to the Gallery's small existing group of mannerist pictures by Heintz, Christoph Schwarz, Rottenhammer and Bartholomaus Dietterlin.

The disappearance of these and other pictures becomes understandable when we learn from the lists of outgoing works drawn up between 1595 and 1610 that the Court painter Zacharias Wehme was commissioned to make copies for the *Kunstkammer* of pictures by Gilles Coignet and Spranger, when the originals were removed by the Electress Hedwiga for her personal use.

In 1588 there was an important acquisition. The inventory mentions 'divers pieces sold to my gracious Lord by Lukas Krannigk, burgess of Torgau.' These were pictures inherited from Lucas Cranach the Younger by his son, who sold them to the Elector.

13

Several of them are still in the Gallery, including *St Catherine* and *St Barbara*, probably painted by the elder Cranach about 1516 (Gal. nos. 1906 E and F) and a series of seven scenes from the life of Christ, by Albrecht Dürer (Gal. nos. 1875–1881). These originally surrounded a central painting of the *Mater Dolorosa* which is now at Munich, in the Alte Pinakothek. Painted between 1496 and 1498, they were attributed for a long time to Dürer's workshop. But in 1956, during restoration in the Dresden Gallery, the coarse over-painting was removed, revealing a delicacy of colour and draughtsmanship which justified the conclusion that they were by Dürer's own hand.

Other pictures acquired from the estate of the younger Cranach were three by Jacopo di Barbari–then known in Germany as Wälsche Jakob ('Italian' Jacob), who had been employed by the Emperor Maximilian from 1500 to 1504 and by Frederick the Wise of Saxony from 1503 to 1505. He had an important influence on the art world of his time, for he helped to carry the principles of Italian Renaissance art into Germany.

One of these paintings, *Christ in Benediction* (Gal. no. 57) was taken by Lucas Cranach the Younger as the subject of a wood-cut. The other two, which are rather smaller, represent *St Catherine* and *St Barbara* (Gal. nos. 58, 59). Purchase prices are only occasionally given in the inventories. One of the entries for 1590 mentions that 'A canvas painted in oil colours showing Queen Sophonisba, her murder by poison, the which was made by the Emperor's painter, Bartholomaeus Spranger, costs 60 Thalers.'

In considering the subsequent development of the *Kunstkammer*, it should be remembered that from 1618 to 1648 the Thirty Years War was ravaging Germany, bringing cultural life almost entirely to a stop, disrupting the economy and reducing the population to a quarter of its former figure.

Even in those troublous times, however, some not inconsiderable purchases were made for the Dresden Gallery.

In 1622, during the reign of Johann Georg I (1585–1656) it acquired the collection left by the Court architect, Johann Maria Nosseni, at his death two years previously. This was valued at 6,961

14

guilders, 9 groschen, 6 pfennigs. To those of the paintings which have now vanished were attached a number of impressive names—Titian, Tintoretto, Sebastiano del Piombo, Parmigianino—but all these, as even the compilers of the old inventory suspected, were probably copies, erroneous attributions or even fakes. The names are worth noting, however, for they hint at the trend of contemporary taste. This incident also shows us that something in the nature of private art galleries already existed in Dresden.

The pictures from Nosseni's collection which were to be seen until recently in the Gallery included two portraits from the Cranach workshop—one of *Luther* and one of *Melanchthon* (Gal. nos. 1918, 1919)—and a woodland scene depicting a pause on the *Flight into Egypt*, from the School of Paul Bril. This last, however, perished in the second World War.

The steady intake of new items had gradually filled the *Kunstkammer* to overflowing. The picture section must have been particularly crowded. We have to realize that, the available wall space being long since exhausted, the paintings were stacked or rolled up and left in cupboards—the congestion being at its worst after the arrival of large consignments, such as Nosseni's or the entire artistic legacy of the Court painter Zacharias Wehme (acquired in 1608) with its numerous portraits and biblical scenes, some of them unfinished, together with hunting scenes by other painters.

As a temporary solution, a number of objects were bundled together on shelves and in cupboards. Moreover many exhibits had been removed; but the gaps they left had to be kept free, however reluctantly this was done, as it was impossible to foresee if and when any of them would be restored to the collection.

The necessity for a drastic rearrangement finally became clear—a rearrangement which in the event dragged on until 1610 and, where the reserves were concerned, until 1619. No change was made in the general principles on which the arrangement was based, although the order of the different rooms was altered, so that generally speaking the *Kunstkammer* still conformed to the type described by Neickel at the beginning of the eighteenth century. But the collection kept

15

on growing, until it became the practice to discard pieces that had lost their value or been damaged. Finally, Inspector Brunn drew up a plan for the entire rearrangement of the collection, entailing more space. When Brunn died in 1628 the work was still unfinished; his successor, Theodor Häsel, managed to complete it in 1640. The inventory he made at this time refers to one hundred pictures all traces of which were lost long ago. Brunn made improvements in the system, to the advantage of the pictures as well as the rest of the collection. Paintings were now grouped by subjects—royal portraits were hung in one room, religious scenes in another, with two further rooms for historical episodes and two for animal pictures. A final and favourite corner room was reserved for portraits of the Electors of Saxony together with twelve oil paintings and a like number of plaster casts of the earliest Roman emperors—giving proper emphasis to the dynastic connection. A further step towards the proper organization of the collection had thus been taken.

After Häsel's death (1658), Tobias Beutel was put in charge of the Dresden *Kunstkammer*. A new period of expansion began with the

LUCAS CRANACH THE YOUNGER (1515–1586)   ▷
AUGUSTUS I, ELECTOR OF SAXONY
Gallery No. 1947, Cardboard, 40×32.5 cm.

Augustus I, Elector of Saxony from 1553 to 1586, was the founder of the Dresden *Kunstkammer*. It outgrew its premises, and the paintings that formed the nucleus of the picture gallery were selected from this source in 1707. A full-length, official-looking portrait of this ruler, by Lucas Cranach the Younger, hangs in the hunting-box of Moritzburg, near Dresden. The portrait shown here, from the Dresden Gallery itself, is less formal in its appearance and makes a more direct appeal. The broad, strong head, with the rather fleshy face framed in short hair and a reddish beard, suggests a combination of energy and circumspection.

The output from Cranach's workshop, where this picture was produced, grew to considerable proportions, so that sometimes the quality of the individual paintings suffered. Nevertheless, this portrait shows what fine work could still be produced during the latter part of the sixteenth century.

The picture probably came from the *Kunstkammer* into the Gallery in 1707, though it does not appear in the catalogue until 1835.

16

arrival of this versatile, cultivated man, who also pursued scientific and literary interests. To purchase merely such works of art as made their appearance locally was no longer considered adequate, so agents set out on their travels with authority to buy suitable pieces. Domenico Melani, Privy Chamberlain to the Elector of Saxony, *Oberlandbaumeister* Wolf Caspar Klengel, and the painter Samuel Bottschild all visited Italy and Greece and returned to Dresden with works of art (or what, for lack of experience, they believed to be such). This was the first attempt to escape from local shackles. The Elector himself (Georg III, 1647–1691) also travelled abroad, and brought back pictures from Venice for his collection.

The catalogue kept by Beutel from 1658 to 1688 includes an increasing number of pictures still to be seen in the Gallery. One of the entries for 1659 mentions that 'On 15th October Klengel brought in an Italian painting (ascribed to Rubenio), a love-tragedy of Hero and Leander, which the Well-Beloved Consort of His Highness the Elector (Georg II, 1613–1680) ordered to be placed in the *Kunstkammer*, it measures 4 ells all but a quarter in width and 2 ells all but a quarter in height, is surrounded by strips of white wood and was hung on the wall of the fourth room, to the left side of the entrance.'

In 1687 we read again: 'On 7th November, by Bottschild, 12 valuable rare paintings, the most of them old: 1) A piece from Ovid, of Hero and Leander, how Leander swam to Hero across the sea, Hero awaiting him upon a cliff, but he being drowned in a storm at sea, she likewise, in the pain of her heart, fell down from the cliff and lost her life. This picture is 2 ells in width and 5/4 ells in height, in a plain frame. Notandum: The same was brought back from Venice by His Highness the Elector himself. And though His Highness may indeed have a like painting of larger size in his *Kunstkammer* already, yet this now brought back is the true original, painted by Peter Paul Rubenssen, of Antwerp, but the other a mere Copy, that now brought being of much older colours, and more gracefully painted, the other not so good, and in newer, fresher colours.'

The picture delivered by Klengel has been in Dresden ever since

17

(Gal. no. 1002). In the catalogue of the subsequently opened Art Gallery, drawn up in 1741, it appears as no. 35 with the description 'painted in the style of Rubens, but not an original.' For this reason it was withdrawn from exhibition and kept in the *Kunstkammer* until 1832. Not until 1860 did it reappear in the Gallery, and it was still regarded for a long time as a workshop product.

The smaller version (acquired by Georg III in 1687) was one of the paintings selected by Augustus the Strong for his new picture gallery. In the latter half of the eighteenth century it was sold, however, perhaps owing to uncertainty as to its attribution. After considerable wanderings it found its way into a private collection in England, and is still there. The picture remaining in Dresden is thought to be a rather later version, painted by the Master himself with a few slight changes, of the earlier picture, which he painted about 1606 in Rome or Genoa.

Considerable additions were made to the Cranach section of the *Kunstkammer* during Beutel's term of office. Nevertheless, a number of the pictures acquired at that time are now considered to be no more than products of Cranach's studio (Gal. nos. 1923, 1925, 1927, 1928, 1929, 1934, 1935 and 1936, all of which have been in the collection since 1657).

In 1676 the *Portrait of a Man with Three Arrows* (Gal. no. 842) was brought from the fortress of Königstein; painted by an unknown Dutch master about the year 1500, it is attributed in the inventory to Lucas van Leyden.

An important event, the repercussions of which were not felt until much later, occurred in the very year (1687) when Georg III brought back the first version of the *Hero and Leander* from Italy to Dresden. Two pictures are recorded. One of them is 'with closed case or wings, more than $2^1/_4$ ells in height and over 2 ells in width, the outer side of the wings being adorned with the swords and garlands of the House of Saxony, and within is Mary with the Christ-child and pictures of angels; on the one wing the aged Joseph, on the other the bent head and shoulders of a praying Christian, but the whole painted merely in water-colours on thin canvas stretched over wood, damaged

18

in parts, *incerti autoris*. The said two pictures having been removed by His Serene Highness the Elector from his castle church at Wittenberg and brought hither, that the Court painter Samuel Bottschilden may here make copies and the copies be given to Wittenberg.'

The *autor incertus* was Albrecht Dürer, who had painted the Dresden altarpiece for Frederick the Wise about 1496 (Gal. no. 1869). Beutel reveals himself as a somewhat unreliable iconographer when he takes the St Anthony on the left-hand panel of the triptych for Joseph and fails to recognize the 'bent head and shoulders of a praying Christian' as a St Sebastian.

It is remarkable that Dürer's name was already forgotten by this time, though the altarpiece in the Castle church at Wittenberg had always been acknowledged to be by him. Even in 1835, when the picture was brought from the reserve into the Gallery, there was uncertainty as to who had painted it. Matthäi's catalogue of that year enters it among the pictures of the German School as by an unknown master. Later, only the side-panels were attributed to the Nuremberg artist. Doubts as to the authenticity of the attribution to Dürer persisted until the turn of the century, and were not finally set at rest till Ludwig Justi published his monograph, *Dürers Dresdner Altar*, in 1904.

The other work entered in the inventory for 1687 at the same time as this one was also an altarpiece, 'having within how Christ was taken prisoner by night and restored Malchus's severed ear, and on the outer side two holy women with goblet and sword, painted by Lucas van Leyden.' This is now thought to be the work of an unknown Dutch master, of about 1500, possibly Jan Joos van Kalkar (Gal. no. 841). The two side panels were sold in the middle of the eighteenth century, and brought back to the Gallery in 1876 from the *Gotische Haus* at Wörlitz through an exchange. Among other paintings added to the *Kunstkammer* during the same period, mention should be made of *David and Goliath*, by Jan van Scorel (Gal. no. 844, in the collection since 1691), works by Valckenborch, Pignoni and Paudiss (Gal. nos. 832, 507, 1993 and 1996), and Rubens' *Drunken Hercules* (Gal. no. 987), which was acquired during the

19

reign of Johann Georg IV (1668–1694), probably direct from the artist's estate. Later, in 1743, a copy of this picture, made in the Rubens workshop, was acquired for the Gallery by Rossi in Mantua, together with a replica of *The Paragon*, the original of which is now in the Alte Pinakothek in Munich (Gal. nos. 956, 957).

Generally speaking, the pictures admitted to the *Kunstkammer* between 1560 and 1694 (the year in which Georg IV died) are not very impressive. Side by side with a swarm of royal portraits and hunting or historical pieces by Dresden painters – Wehme, Goeding, Roder, Bretschneider and Schürer – came 'rare paintings by famous masters which would certainly not have borne closer inspection, attributed as they were to Titian, Tintoretto, Sebastiano del Piombo or Raphael. They have vanished, like the works of the mannerists, Spranger, Coignet and Parmigianino.

The large representation of Cranach and his workshop was an outstanding feature of the Saxon *Kunstkammer*, whereas the value of some highly important pieces by early German painters was not recognized until later. This is made particularly clear by the treatment accorded Albrecht Dürer's Dresden altarpiece, and by the long neglect of the three paintings by Jacopo di Barbari which were acquired from the estate of Lucas Cranach the Younger.

The presence of small paintings by Hans Bol, Valckenborch and Henri met de Bles gives early indication of a special interest in purely artistic values. But the only really significant items to have been acquired deliberately are the two paintings by Rubens, *Hero and Leander* and the *Drunken Hercules*.

The Dresden *Kunstkammer*, then, owed its fame – spread abroad by travelling writers – not so much to paintings as to treasures of other types. There are no reports on the collection until 1600, for in earlier years visits to the rooms were prohibited, and even later it was difficult to gain admission. Fear of theft may have been the chief reason for the security regulations. The severity with which thieves were treated is exemplified by the sentence passed on Wolf Stübichen, a locksmith employed to put new locks on the doors in October 1623. He kept skeleton keys, let himself into the *Kunstkammer* and stole

20

a few valuable objects. He was caught, and hanged in Dresden on 13th January 1624.

As the seventeenth century wore on, however, it gradually became the custom to show the treasures of the *Kunstkammer* not only to royal guests visiting the Court of Saxony, but to passing travellers as well. The gratuities they paid were no doubt shared out between the custodian and his staff. The use to which the money was put is specified in the commission granted to Tobias Beutel in 1658. He was to receive a yearly salary of 200 guilders, with an extra 25 guilders as dress allowance. His predecessor Häsel, who died in 1658, had not fared so well. He complained in a petition to the Elector that his salary had not been paid for 8 years; this meant that he had to fall back on tips, which, since visitors were still infrequent, did not amount to much. Beutel's letter of appointment also explains the usual method of showing visitors round. After a precise explanation of who is to carry the keys and admit the visitors, it runs: 'If any persons declare their wish to visit the *Kunstkammer*, our aforementioned *Oberlandbaumeister* shall be informed, and the said persons shall be carefully noted and, with his permission and on his order, led through the *Kunstkammer*, great caution being observed to ensure that among so many people, no object shall be lost; moreover, any matter entrusted to him he shall keep to himself in silence to the grave, revealing nothing thereof to any man.'

The number of visitors increased considerably during Beutel's term of office, for the Grand Tour was already becoming an institution for young princes. The development of the Dresden art collection itself received appreciable stimulus as a result of these educational tours. In 1671 Beutel wrote his *Cedern-Wald*, a kind of guidebook for his guests, providing summary information about the Dresden collection and other local items of interest. This mentions not only the *Kunstkammer*, but other, separate collections – the 'Saddleroom' and 'Armoury', the 'Library', and the 'Anatomical Cabinet', which were already receiving, from time to time, the overflow from the crowded *Kunstkammer*.

The descriptions given in the *Cedern-Wald* are very brief, forming

21

little more than an inventory. It is clear from them that the atmosphere of the old 'cabinets of art and curiosities' still prevailed, an impression confirmed by Anton Weck, the author of a travel book published in Nuremberg in 1680, who remarks that 'Indeed, this *Kunstkammer* is so extensive and filled with such an abundance of rarities and marvels, that it is rather to be admired than to be described or adequately appraised.'

Tobias Beutel, the custodian, died in 1690. Until 1739 his post was filled by a nephew of the same name. The *Kunstkammer* had lost its real importance by this time, for radical changes had already taken place and were to culminate in its closing down in 1832. Items worth keeping were brought together with others from the Armoury to form a Historical Museum, the remaining ones were sold by auction in 1835. For the past hundred years and more, the centre of gravity of the Dresden art collection had lain elsewhere.

ORIGIN OF THE PICTURE GALLERY

On 25th March 1701, the *Georgenbau* of the Elector's Palace at Dresden was destroyed by fire. Among the portions burnt out was the celebrated *Hall of the Giants*, decorated in 1625 and the years following with a series of views of Saxon towns, painted by Wilhelm Dilich, the topographer and builder of fortifications. The rooms composing the *Kunstkammer* were undamaged, but steps were immediately taken to move their contents elsewhere, as a precaution. The removal gave occasion for a rearrangement of the entire inventory, which also helped to prepare the way for dividing the collection into separate museums. These events thus mark the first step towards the formation of an independent picture gallery.

The fire was merely the ostensible reason for this innovation, however. Its real causes lay deeper. The old-style *Kunstkammer* had long ceased to satisfy the requirements of princely display. The new age, set upon presenting a brilliant front, needed more elbow-room than was provided by the narrow walls of a 'Cabinet of Curiosities'. And no one was more disposed to make full use of the available resources for his own ends than the Elector Frederick Augustus I of Saxony, known as 'the Strong' when he became King of Poland (1670–1733).

Augustus came to the throne in 1694, at the age of twenty-four, on the untimely death of his brother Johann Georg IV. Bursting with ambition, he immediately set himself to bring his far-reaching plans to fruition, and so win a place for Saxony (which in those days of absolute monarchy meant, in practice, for its ruler) second to none among the great European powers. He was a ruthless egoist, but his incredible vitality, unaccompanied though it was by any intellectual discipline, his activity, however basically inconsistent, and his riotous imagination, which blinded him to practical possibilities, have something impressive about them until we realize the formlessness of his whole career, and how few of his vast projects ever materialized. The vestiges that remain are impressive enough, but should not blind us the tremendous burden they laid, not on the ruler himself, but on his people. Frederick Augustus I was determined to secure the throne of Poland. He allowed no obstacles to deter him from this political ambition. On one occasion he did not scruple to drain the State coffers of Saxony by taking out of them the huge sums he needed for bribing the Polish electors. Another time, in order to make himself eligible for election, he became a Roman Catholic, utterly disregarding the strong Protestant tradition of Saxony and of his own house. He smoothed over all misgivings, and in 1697 actually got himself elected. The adventure was followed, however, by a temporary setback. In 1704, after the King's unskilful conduct of the war with Charles XII of Sweden, the Polish parliament deposed him, and the terms of the Peace of Altranstädt, in 1706, obliged him to abdicate officially. Meanwhile, Stanislas Leszczynski had been elected to the throne in Warsaw. But after Charles XII was defeated at Poltava in 1709 the crown was again bestowed on Augustus.

This raised Dresden to the rank of a European capital, and despite the Altranstädt fiasco Augustus was still considered important enough to fill the high office of *Reichsvikar* when the Emperor Joseph I died in 1711. He also succeeded in consolidating the power of his family by concluding influential alliances with other dynastic houses; in 1719 his son's marriage to the Emperor's daughter, Maria Josepha of Austria, took place in Dresden. From the political standpoint, however, the connection did not produce the expected results.

These ambitious projects needed a brilliant presentation against a magnificently effective background, to enhance their importance and engender respect.

Making the Grand Tour in France, Spain and Italy between 1687 and 1689, the young heir to the Saxon throne had seen for himself what a self-respecting ruler's household should be like. Like many German princes of that day, he had received his strongest and most lasting impression at the Court of Louis XIV at Versailles, while in Italy, Venice had cast its spelt over him. Sensitive to the subtle fascination of that unique blend of art and nature, to the beauty of the palaces

24

romantically mirrored in the water of the canals, the prince formed a clear idea of what his native city must acquire before it could have a voice in the European concert. And on his unexpected accession to the throne he immediately set himself to put his plans into practice in this as in other respects. Not content with mere details, he strove to set up an organization incorporating the widest possible range of arts. The fortifications that hemmed in the cramped sixteenth-century Residence were broken through on the side nearest to the River Elbe, and within a few decades had taken on the picturesque aspect made familiar to later generations by Bernardo Bellotto's pictures of it. Various palaces were built and parks laid out, including Pillnitz, Moritzburg and Grosssedlitz; but it was the Zwinger, constructed in 1709 by Daniel Pöppelmann and the stucco artist Balthasar Permoder, which provided the ideal setting for the prodigally lavish ceremonies attending the marriage of the Elector's heir apparent and the Emperor's daughter.

The demands of royal pomp were not satisfied by a Residence composed of magnificent buildings; it was equally important to display a valuable art collection. It was *Oberlandbaumeister* Baron Raymond Le Plat (1664–1742), interior decorator to the Saxon Court since 1698, who persuaded Augustus the Strong to rearrange his art collections in the style adopted long before at Versailles. Le Plat's ideas were after the Elector's own heart, and received a ready welcome. He first turned his attention to the purchase of classical sculpture, of which there was none in Dresden at that time. It proved possible to buy 32 statues from Cardinal Albani of Rome, and to acquire two other Italian collections – the Chigi and the Bellori – which included a number of masterpieces such as the Athena Lemnia, the *Wine-pouring Satyr* by Praxiteles, and Polycleitus' *Victorious Boy*,

King Augustus' passion for East Asian porcelain is well known. After 1709, when Johann Friedrich Böttger discovered the secret of manufacturing porcelain, the King encouraged the new industry by placing orders with the first European factory, at Meissen, not far from Dresden, to supplement his large purchases from China.

Money was squandered for this purpose with unparalleled reckless-

25

ness. Augustus the Strong and his successor, Augustus III (1696–1763), could not, however, have carried out even a fraction of their schemes without an industrious and efficient middle class to provide the necessary economic and financial conditions. When money ran short, soldiers were bartered. For instance, in the year 1717, after lengthy negotiations, King Frederick William I of Prussia accepted 600 dragoons in exchange for a batch of large Chinese vases, several of which are still in the Dresden collection of porcelain and are known in popular parlance as the 'Dragoon vases'.

Augustus the Strong was fond of paintings as well as of china. While on the Grand Tour he had already begun to buy pictures, and his choice was entirely governed by his own individual taste. He was an amateur, of the kind first exemplified in modern art collecting by the Duc de Berry, and the amateur is invariably conspicuous for his subjectivity. Even the most individualistic collector is influenced by the style of his period; but some styles leave more scope for personal predilections than do others. The grand manner promoted by the early eighteenth century was specially propitious to the subjective outlook of the amateur, for its tendency towards brilliant exaggeration tallied with the collector's propensity to use art as a means of setting off his own personality. He could assemble everything that served this end –things noble or magnificent, ingenious or gay, colourful and dramatic, intoxicatingly and overwhelmingly beautiful; in short, the art of the High Renaissance as well as Italian and Flemish Baroque.

The late nineteenth century, revering the spirit of History, based its collections on far more objective principles, which were alleged to lead to perfection. The history of art was to be illustrated as fully as possible by carefully selected masterpieces. Characteristic of this period is its invention of the science museum, so radically different from the galleries of the Baroque age.

It is quite possible, of course, for collecting on these lines to be motivated by the most happy impulses. But if one may be somewhat critical, the satisfaction it engenders is liable to proceed not so much from the actual ownership of beautiful or fascinating objects as from the joy of having, by dint of effort and sacrifice, 'covered' a particular

26

field. Many a rare item which does not appeal to the collector's personal taste has to be acquired simply for the sake of completeness. Considerations of this kind were entirely alien to Augustus the Strong and the men of his period, who loved beauty for its own sake. Carl Justi, in his book on Winckelmann and his contemporaries, says very rightly that 'the need to delight in beauty made this the classical period for art galleries.'

Field Marshal von Flemming, who had been responsible for acquiring several pictures for the Dresden collection, once described his sovereign in the following words: 'His ruling passions are enjoyment and the pursuit of glory, but enjoyment comes first; his ambition has often been thwarted by his love of pleasure, but the reverse has never happened.' This description also applies to King Augustus's activities as a collector, for what he enjoyed was to enhance his fame by indulging his love of beauty amid the masterpieces he assembled in such extravagant quantities.

As heir apparent, he began by purchasing works by the lesser Dutch masters of the seventeenth century. While still on his Grand Tour he acquired paintings by Jan Brueghel the Elder, 'Velvet Brueghel' (Gal. nos. 893, 894; in the inventory of 1722 they are marked 'from Italy, through the Elector's heir').

After Le Plat's advent at the Court of Saxony (1698) there was a sharp rise in picture-buying. Among the most important acquisitions during this period were fifteen paintings sold to the King by the Paris art dealer Le Roy; they included Giorgione's *Sleeping Venus* (Gal. no. 185) and Gillis van Coninxloo's *Landscape with the Judgment of Midas* (Gal. no. 587), the significance of which lies in that it is an early example of landscape painting as an independent branch of art.

In March 1700 Samuel Rottschild delivered 342 pictures for the *Kunstkammer*. Many of these disappeared long ago and cannot even be identified. The most important of the surviving items is the small painting of a pair of lovers by Metsu (Gal. no. 1732), a picture whose resemblance to Rembrandt's self-portrait with Saskia on his knee (Gal. no. 1559) has recently prompted the suggestion that this too is a self-portrait. The coincidence of theme is at all events surprising.

27

After being rearranged several times since the fire of 1701, the *Kunstkammer* had once more become hopelessly overcrowded as a result of all these additions, and Augustus the Strong felt that it was time to afford his treasures a more up-to-date and spacious display. Le Plat inspected the entire royal collection, and on his advice a list of 535 pictures was drawn up by Tobias Beutel, curator of the *Kunstkammer*, and signed by Heinrich Christoph Fehling, the inspector of paintings. It is headed 'Specification of those Paintings which His Royal Majesty the Most Gracious Elector of Saxony has been graciously pleased to permit to be removed from his Cabinet and placed and arranged in the Ballroom and the other rooms, Anno 1707, this 28th day of February.'

It seems clear that the decision was taken at this particular time because in 1707, after the Swedish troops had been withdrawn from Saxony, Augustus the Strong had moved his residence from Warsaw to Dresden and begun to take a keen interest in the embellishment of his surroundings.

Beutel's list may be regarded as the birth-certificate of the Dresden Gallery, though the new arrangement was not an art gallery in the strict meaning of the term. The pictures were merely selected to decorate some of the state apartments where the monarchs and their guests assembled on the occasion of great receptions.

The original meaning of the word 'gallery' was not a collection of pictures but a long, narrow and magnificent room connecting two other groups of apartments in a palace. Such a room, with light flooding in through the row of windows along one side, made an excellent setting for works of art. Galleries were used for the display of pictures in French *châteaux* as early as the seventeenth century. Not until later was the name of the room transferred to its contents. The classical example of this is the *Grande Galerie* of the Louvre in Paris, which is several hundred yards in length. Smaller and more personal collections were still kept in 'cabinets', a word often used even nowadays for displays of coins or engravings.

But although in 1707 the Dresden pictures were not hung in true 'gallery style', this is not the important point. The interesting aspect

28

of the matter is that the contents of the *Kunstkammer* were for the first time successfully divided up. This was something fundamentally novel, out of which all later developments proceeded only gradually. The lists of acquisitions for this period mention works by Dou, Mieris, Wouwerman, Berchem, Griffier, Saftleven, Poelenburgh, Mignon, Bloemaert, Rubens, Van Dyck, Teniers, Rembrandt, Schönfeld, Elsheimer, Heintz, and a number of Italians, including Dolci, Reni, Vecchia, Pietro da Cortona and Sassoferrato.

The most important of the pictures proposed for the ballroom and neighbouring rooms were Giorgione's *Sleeping Venus*, the *Drunken Hercules* by Rubens, and a number of works by Lucas Cranach (which seems, for that epoch, a rather unexpected homage to the *genius loci*). Many smaller landscapes and genre paintings by lesser seventeenth-century Dutch and Flemish masters were also selected.

An extensive network of middlemen and agents took care that the flow of pictures into the collection would not dry up. Baron Le Plat was still in charge of operations at Dresden. One of the outstanding works he secured for the Gallery was Poussin's *Kingdom of Flora* (Gal. no. 719). Others who were actively buying up pictures were Field Marshal von Flemming, Count Wackerbarth, and the Court painters, Rottschild and Louis de Silvestre. Antoine Pesne and Balthasar Denner were the King's agents in Berlin and Hamburg respectively. Pictures were bought at the Leipzig Fair as well, including Aert de Gelder's *Halberdier* (Gal. no. 1792).

Dresden already had connections extending far beyond the bounds of the German States. We have already mentioned the business relationship with the Paris art dealer Le Roy. Antwerp was another large centre for dealings in pictures, which is not surprising in view of King Augustus's partiality for small Dutch and Flemish paintings. The art dealers Lemmers and de Wit were established there, and from them the Dresden collection acquired a number of pictures, including *Return of Diana from the Hunt*, by Peter Paul Rubens (Gal. no. 962 A), the large *Ariadne and Bacchus*, by Jordaens (Gal. no. 1009), and the *Still-life with Birds' Nest*, by Jan Davidsz. de Heem, which later became famous (Gal. no. 1261). The already large group of works

29

by Wouwerman was augmented by further purchases. This painter seems to have aroused and maintained considerable interest at Dresden, for today still there are thirty-eight of his pictures in the collection.

Graf von Wackerbarth, a member of the Privy Council, brought in two important works by Van Dyck, dating from 1618, when the painter was still under the influence of his master, Rubens,—the portrait of an *Old Man* and, as its companion piece, the portrait of an *Old Woman* (Gal. nos. 1022, 1023)—and a typical work by Gerard ter Borch, *Lady washing her Hands* (Gal. no. 1830), one of the most valuable examples of Dutch genre painting in the Dresden Gallery. Salomon Koninck contributed *The Hermit* (erroneously attributed to Rembrandt) and a number of pictures by Berchem.

There were fewer purchases of Italian works now. The preference was for large, decorative, picturesque paintings. The Gallery acquired two pictures—*Bacchus and Ariadne* (Gal. no. 572) and *The Rape of Europa* (Gal. no. 573)—by the Venetian painter Francesco Migliori, who was still living, and works by Liberi, Celesti and Giordano. Francesco Albani's *Galatea in her Shell Chariot* (Gal. no. 340) achieved some degree of celebrity when Johann Joachim Kändler took it as the theme for decorating the lid of a dish in his Meissen 'Swan' service (1737–1741).

Rather lost among so many showy and impressive items was a little quattrocento painting by Cima da Conegliano, a grave *Head of Christ*, full of character (Gal. no. 62). Looking at the list of pictures acquired during the two decades immediately following the accession of Augustus the Strong, we notice the marked preponderance of good paintings by seventeenth-century Dutch and Flemish masters. Thus, the foundations of the collection of pictures from the Netherlands to which the Dresden Gallery still owes much of its reputation were laid during those years.

But all this was no more than a prelude. The golden age came in the following decades.

30

THE GOLDEN AGE

No type of building reflects the artistic structure of the period around 1700 more clearly than do the Baroque palaces of which Versailles was the supreme example. The period of absolute monarchy, with its rigid social hierarchy, found its architectural expression in a system of town-planning which set the palace of the sovereign in the same central position that he himself occupied in the State. All the principal roads lead to it, while from the gardens at the rear the paths and avenues radiate out into the boundless contryside. Moreover, the dominating position of the royal residence is emphasized by the surrounding smaller buildings—chapel, theatre, library, museum—which in any other form of social organization would play an independent part on their own merits.

It is an odd fact that no such royal precincts ever took shape at Dresden, although the circumstances after the fire of 1701 might seem highly propitious, and despite the unprecedented building activity that went on in the town up to the middle of the century. Many private mansions were built in these years by the aristocracy and the prosperous middle class, in addition to Pöppelmann's vast Zwinger project, the Catholic church with its slender, open-work, almost Gothic-looking tower, erected for the Court by Gaetano Chiaveri, and the massive *Frauenkirche* with its bell-shaped dome, built for the Protestants to the design of Georg Bähr, master-builder to the Council. Extensive plans for a new palace were prepared, and would certainly have satisfied the ambitious schemes of Augustus the Strong. Pöppelmann, for instance, prepared a project for a building in conjunction with the Zwinger, which was to stand right on the riverbank. But none of these proposals materialized. Probably their execution was beyond the powers of those who would have had to carry them out, so that what already existed was deemed sufficient. Besides, large buildings were actually put up outside Dresden—the castle at

31

Pillnitz, on the Elbe, and the hunting-box of Moritzburg, north of the city – which reduced the need for a new Residence.

This state of things influenced the subsequent development of the picture gallery. The removal of the paintings from the *Kunstkammer* in 1701 had been the first step towards an independent collection. But the cramped sixteenth-century Electoral Palace could provide no place for a properly impressive gallery, such as might have been housed in a spacious, well-designed Baroque building.

Things were different in Bavaria, where the majority of the most important paintings hung in the 'Grande Galerie' in the palace of Schleissheim until 1780/81, when the Elector Carl Theodor had a separate building erected for them in Munich itself – the *Hofgartengalerie*, to which the most valuable of the pictures from Schleissheim and other royal seats were transferred. A special gallery to house the pictures at Kassel was built half-way through the century (1749–

HYACINTHE RIGAUD (1659–1743)　　　　　　　　　　　　　　　　　▷
AUGUSTUS III AS HEIR APPARENT
Gallery No. 760, Canvas, 250×173 cm.

Some portrait painters have an instinctive talent for giving their sitters exactly the appearance that fashionable society of the day regards as the ideal. The type recurs in every period; the perfect example in the seventeenth century was Van Dyck, and in the nineteenth, artists such as Sargent or Lenbach. During the first half of the eighteenth century Hyacinthe Rigaud filled this role; not for nothing had his taste been formed by his early study of Van Dyck.

Rigaud was painter to five kings. The pattern for his whole output is the large picture of Louis XIV, painted in 1701, which now hangs in the Louvre. This portrait of Augustus, heir to the throne of Saxony, which was painted in Paris in 1715, conforms to the same tradition. The 19-year-old Prince is shown in an attitude of command, his right hand grasping his Field-Marshal's baton. So much grandeur is hardly in keeping with the personality of Augustus III, as recorded by history. In vigour and prudence he was much inferior to his father, Augustus the Strong, and he proved to be no match for his rival, Frederick the Great. His passion for collecting works of art was a serious danger to the national economy. But his name is associated with the most important acquisitions made by the Dresden Gallery in the middle decades of the eighteenth century, culminating in the purchase of Raphael's *Sistine Madonna*. Rigaud himself delivered his portrait of Augustus III to the Gallery, and it appears in the inventory for 1722.

32

1751) to the design of François Cuvilliés, while Berlin had the Potsdam Gallery, erected in 1756 at the order of Frederick II, in the vicinity of his Sanssouci Palace.

For the reasons already given, a solution of this kind had to be sought at Dresden at a much earlier date. In 1722 a general inventory of all pictures in the King's possession—in the *Kunstkammer* and in the different churches and palaces—reached an already impressive total; it had risen, when the inventory was revised in 1742, to over 4,700. The ballroom and the neighbouring apartments in the Residence had long been insufficient for the display of even the principal works in the collection. In 1722, under Le Plat's supervision, the most valuable items were set aside and removed to the so-called 'stables'. The Dresden collection at last had its own premises, where it was to remain until 1855.

These formed part of a group bordering the Judenhof and built in the last quarter of the sixteenth century. A long, arcaded building set against the inner wall of the city connected the palace with the actual stables. Many splendid tournaments and other displays were held there. In the eighteenth century, however, such performances were given in the Zwinger instead.

The stables comprised four buildings opening on to a rectangular courtyard. The first floor was allocated to the pictures and the available space increased by adding a low-ceilinged attic storey, the old Renaissance pediments being demolished for this purpose. In 1729 a horseshoe-shaped flight of outside steps and a pediment decorated with the arms of Saxony and Poland were added to the façade overlooking the Judenhof, which is shown in Bellotto's painting. At this time there were small, balcony-like abutments projecting from the bevelled corners of the building. Regardless of the new use to which the *belle étage* was being put, the ground floor continued to serve as stabling and coach-house until 1794, when new stables, with a riding-school, were built near the Zwinger. It thus became possible, in that same year, to unpack the famous Mengs collection of casts of antique statues from the chests in which it had been hidden away until then, and arrange it in the liberated premises.

33

Le Plat was still chief curator of the Gallery, with 'Privy Chamberlain' Steinhäuser in charge of technical and administrative matters. He kept the inventory up to date and his entries show further interesting acquisitions in the years preceding the death of Augustus the Strong (1733). By this time Venice, as well as Antwerp, was an important centre for buyers from Dresden. The painter Lorenzo Rossi lived there as the King's agent from 1724 to 1728. He was instrumental in adding a fresh group of works by contemporary Italian artists to the collection, as well as the *Sleeping Venus* by Palma Vecchio (Gal. no. 190), often regarded as an earthy companion-piece to Giorgione's *Venus* with its classical repose. In 1725 Le Plat acquired another fine picture by Palma, the *Holy Family* (Gal. no. 191); Bernardo Strozzi's *Rebecca at the Well* (Gal. no. 656) was bought at the same time. Outstanding among the French purchases was Grimou's *Flute Player* (Gal. no. 772).

From the point of view of quality, however, the Netherlands school was still to the fore. Here the principal new item was Rembrandt's *Samson's Wedding* (Gal. no. 1560), mentioned in the inventory for 1722 with no indication as to how it was acquired. The same inventory mentions Rembrandt's *Self-portrait with Sketchbook* (Gal. no. 1569), a second version of which is now in the De Young Memorial Museum, San Francisco. The number of pictures by Van Dyck was raised to eight by the arrival of his early *Drunken Silenus* (Gal. no. 1017), and we again find the names of de Heem, Flinck, Teniers and Berchem—the latter being represented by his *Reception of the Moorish Envoy* (Gal. no. 1479).

In 1723 Le Plat acquired from Countess Wrczowecz of Prague the copy made by Rubens, in his youth, of the *Leda and the Swan* which is said to have been painted by Michelangelo for the Duke of Ferrara.

Thus it was that by the time Augustus III came to the throne, in 1733, the picture gallery could well sustain comparison with other valuable collections of the period.

The tremendous progress achieved in these years is more easily understood if we consider collecting as one aspect of the artistic, cultural and social life of that day, bearing in mind the leading role played by the aristocracy and the influence of the Catholic Church.

Unlike Protestantism, Catholicism has always been well disposed towards art, thus providing an extensive field of activity for painters and sculptors. The exceptionally strong attraction of the plastic arts for each of the two Kings of Saxony is partly explained by the presence of this Catholic intellectual attitude, which naturally influenced the development of their picture gallery as well.

In a Protestant atmosphere they could scarcely have indulged their love of collecting to such an extent. The Protestant concern for inner purification, for soul-searching, which in the case of the Calvinists led to a complete ban on everything pictorial, gave little encouragement to the fine arts, and none to those feasts for the eyes in which the age of Baroque delighted.

The original *Kunstkammer* of Augustus I of Saxony is a typical illustration of the Protestant spirit prevailing at his Court at the end of the sixteenth century, as may be seen if we contrast it with the lavish collection formed by Rudolf II of Habsburg.

The conversion of the royal family of Saxony to Catholicism had a further effect on the future of their art gallery, inasmuch as it linked them with an international aristocracy whose network of family connections had led to the development of similar tastes, and created the necessary conditions for an infectious collectors' enthusiasm which took no account of national frontiers. This is even more evident in Augustus III than in Augustus the Strong. Like his father before him, the young heir to the throne had made the Grand Tour and visited Italy, in which country he changed from the Protestant religion in which he had been brought up, to Catholicism. It is true that the son, like the father, was influenced chiefly by political motives; but his willingness to be converted was very likely enhanced by a personal attraction towards the Church of Rome and its dignitaries, with their international outlook and their appreciation of art. Already stimulated by the splendours of his father's Court, the young Prince was most ready to be impressed by the tremendous cultural wealth of Italy vaunted at every stage of his travels by the shrewd and active mentors who guided his steps. He came to regard intellectual pursuits and

35

artistic enjoyment as the natural aim of life. Even after his return to Dresden he refused to change the habits he had acquired, and put the fulfilment of his personal artistic dreams before any of his duties as a monarch. The struggle between duty and inclination, by which his powerful antagonist, Frederick the Great, had been so torn in his youth, was quite unknown to Augustus III.

The character of Augustus was mild, exuberant and rather amorphous. His lack of self-reliance made him a laughing-stock in foreign courts. The official pomp of dress and bearing portrayed in the grand manner in one of Hyacinthe Rigaud's portrait (see page 32), painted in 1715 (Gal. no. 760), was beginning to look rather unconvincing.

The King's one thought was to leave all tiresome affairs of State to Heinrich Brühl, Count of the Holy Roman Empire, a brilliant but ambitious and self-seeking courtier who, completely over-estimating his own abilities, soon brought the country to economic and political ruin.

Brühl felt that his personal dignity required him to have his own art collection, and the Court artists occasionally sought his favour by making copies for him of pictures they had been commissioned to paint. Bernardo Bellotto gave him a complete set of duplicates—in reduced format—of the famous views of Dresden he painted for Augustus III. One of these (Gal. no. 602) shows the row of magnificent buildings erected by the powerful Minister, for his own purposed, on the stretch of the Elbe embankment which was named after him; they included a picture gallery, theatre, library and town house. As a cover for his own expensive hobbies, Brühl took great pains to encourage the ruler's similar propensities. The two men were united in the wish to ensure that 'the lustre of the Polish-Saxon Court should strike the eyes of Ambassadors and other distinguished foreign visitors.' The ineptitude of the attempt to carry on power politics with nothing except brilliant display to back it up was shown by the disastrous outcome of the Seven Years War, when Saxony was defeated by Frederick II. This monarch's views were much more sober. In a letter to an art dealer who was working for him in Paris, he wrote: 'The King in Poland is at liberty to pay 30,000 ducats for one

36

Tableau in that country and to raise 1,000,000 Reichsthalers in Saxony by imposing a poll-tax, but that is not my method. What I can pay for at a reasonable price, I buy, but what is too dear I leave to the King in Poland, for I cannot fabricate money, and it is not for me to impose taxes.'

Thinking of the huge sums paid in those days at Dresden for works of art, we realize that no inconsiderable proportion of the money must have gone into the pockets of the dealers, whom even a man like Frederick II could not by-pass, as the above quotation shows. Many of these shrewd and usually knowledgeable middlemen were aiming at an assured connection with the Court, as the only way of covering the expenses incurred by their fastidious style of living.

In an age when the Welfare State was undreamt of, people without means were haunted by the spectre of poverty. It was only by his own efforts that a man could win an assured position and shake off his apprehensions. Connections and recommendations were of inestimable value. One often forgets that to be obliged to woo the favour of some highly-placed patron with flowery and obsequious professions of friendship may have gone sorely against the grain. But such was the age of rococo. Even Count Algarotti, who travelled frequently between Dresden and Potsdam, did not always escape the sufferings and disappointments of a courtier's life.

Francesco Algarotti was a remarkably intelligent and witty man, who seemed predestined for court life. The son of a Venetian banker, he was born in 1712 and devoted himself at an early age to the extensive studies on which his many-sided and widely-admired culture was based. He shared the proselytising fervour so characteristic of the Enlightenment, and gave vent to it in associating with the highly sophisticated circles which set the fashion at the royal courts of his day. His book, *Newtonianismo per le donne*, written to explain Newton's theory of colours to any ladies who might be interested in the subject, won the approval of such influential men as Voltaire and Fontenelle—much to the satisfaction of the author, who needed their recommendations to forward his career.

Algarotti's life was one long journey from court to court, in the

37

hope that hobnobbing with royalty would culminate in a title, an official post or a pension. After completing his education in Italy he spent some time in Paris and then went to London, whence he travelled to St Petersburg as the companion of Lord Baltimore. On his way back, in 1739, he stopped at Rheinsberg, where he made the acquaintance of the Crown Prince of Prussia, the future Frederick the Great. As soon as he came to the throne, Frederick sent for Algarotti and, fascinated by the Venetian's attractive personality, raised him to the rank of Count, though without fulfilling his hopes of a permanent, salaried post at Court. The assurances of friendship and devotion in Algarotti's letters to the King are often interspersed with complaints that his requests for money have not been met—which is understandable in view of the expense of court life for a man with modest means. Dresden had by now become aware of the *'fameux Algarotti'* and was much disposed to enlist his talents, for a monarch's reputation was enhanced if he succeeded in attracting stars of the first magnitude into his orbit.

In 1742, therefore, the young Count betook himself and his Prussian title to seek better fortune in Saxony. He had not been there long before it was brought home to him how to get on the right side of his new patron, aware as he was of Augustus' enthusiasm for art. He promptly drew up a memorandum which included suggestions for enlarging and improving the royal collections, giving his own extensive knowledge full play. He showed particular skill and tact in calling attention to the gallery's weak points, which he promised to make good with the help of his widespread connections, if he could rely on the Elector's confidence and support.

It is interesting to note that Algarotti also gave his mind to the arrangement of the art collection, and made proposals for a suitably handsome new building to hold them. Typically Italian is his notion of placing the most valuable masterpieces of painting and sculpture in one large room, like the *Tribuna* of the Uffizi in Florence, irrespective of the different schools and periods to which they belong. The Renaissance, with its hero-worshipping tendencies, had been partial to this idea, and it was to be taken up again at Dresden by

38

Gottfried Semper, half-way through the nineteenth century. Even in the early twentieth century the Gallery reverted to the same system, though it was then influenced by the theories of presentation held by the latter-day romantics.

Algarotti did not overlook practical requirements, for he wanted his museum premises—which were to be built on four sides of a quadrangle—to be arranged in simple and logical fashion and properly lighted. Eight domes were to lend dignity to the general outline.

The King and his Minister, Brühl, were greatly impressed. And though the plans for the building were never carried out, Algarotti was able to leave for Italy at the end of February 1743, armed with a list of the King's personal wishes in the matter of pictures, a sum of 1,000 ducats for his own needs, and a supply of letters of credit.

The fatigues and difficulties of the journey itself, the delays attributable to war, plague and long, tedious periods of quarantine—'maledette siano la guerra et la peste' sighs Algarotti in one of his letters—were not then so unusual as we should find them today. Greater strain and exasperation were involved in tracking down the works of art themselves, for many rivals were after the same booty and bent on frustrating one another's efforts. And each failure meant loss of prestige. Time and again an agent's authority would be called in question or his funds prove insufficient, and the bargain he had relied on would elude him at the last moment. There were swindlers, too, always eager to profit by a negotiator's ignorance—selling him pictures with great names to them, which afterwards proved to be forgeries. The agents of Frederick II of Prussia in particular were frequent victims of these charlatans and adventurers.

There was an element of adventure even in the conclusion of a deal. The negotiators went by assumed names, and wore masks when they came to inspect a picture; the process was a kind of secret mission. Algarotti, for example, found to his annoyance that his steps were dogged by another buyer travelling for Brühl, a certain Ventura Rossi. His protests did not elicit proper backing. Worst of all, he was denied the right to call himself 'Surintendant des bâtiments et cabinets du roi', which would have lent the necessary weight to his decisions

39

and which he felt he had earned by his frequently successful efforts. In the end he was fobbed off with the title of Privy Military Counsellor, which added insult to injury, for it had not the remotest connection with his real activities. This called forth mockery from Frederick II, who must have felt a certain malicious satisfaction at the way his former protégé was being treated in Saxony. Thus, despite his many successes, Algarotti's period of work for Dresden ended on a discordant note. He must have been particularly offended when the biggest deal of that period, the purchase of the Duke of Modena's famous collection, was concluded without his help. So in 1747 Algarotti severed his connection with Augustus, Frederick II having offered to take him back to the Prussian Court. The Count's readiness to obey this summons was enhanced by the promise of his long-desired pension – 3,000 thalers – and his admission to the Prussian Order of Merit. Thus he finally had the satisfaction of resigning the military title awarded him by the ungrateful Brühl, and the whole matter was settled with the greatest courtesy on both sides.

Algarotti did not regain any decisive influence over Frederick's art purchases. His health failed, the King granted him leave of absence in 1753, and he spent the remainder of his life in Italy, dying at Pisa in 1764 when only fifty-two years of age.

Thanks to Algarotti, the Dresden Gallery acquired a number of masterpieces and developed the interest in Italian art in general which it had hitherto lacked. Curiously enough, however, it was also he who brought in the first major work of the early German school – *Burgomaster Meyer's Madonna* (Gal. no. 1892), by Hans Holbein the Younger, bought in 1743 from the Delfino family at Venice for the large sum of 1,000 sequins. This was only a masterly seventeenth-century copy, but as the original picture was not then known, and the technique of art criticism was still in its infancy, that was something Algarotti could not be expected to recognize.

What is much more important is the great respect in which he held sixteenth-century German art in general. In his Dresden memorandum he had already set the names of Dürer and Holbein beside those of Italian Renaissance painters, and when discussing the artistic value

40

of a picture he often invoked Holbein as a standard by which to judge. He declared that the two still-lifes by Jan Weenix from the Casa Rumieri in Venice (Gal. nos. 1666, 1667) were 'in their own fashion, two Holbeins' and even praised Liotard's *Chocolate Girl* (Gal. no. P 161) which he bought in Venice in 1745 from the artist himself for 120 sequins, as 'a Holbein in pastel'.

His principal Italian acquisitions included the *Girl with a Viola*, by Bernardo Strozzi, from the Casa Sagredo in Venice (Gal. no. 658), two small pictures by Sebastiano Ricci, *Sacrifice to Vesta* and *Sacrifice to Silenus* (Gal. nos. 549, 550), and the *Three Sisters* by Palma Vecchio (Gal. no. 189), a celebrated picture whose *morbidezza* and *sfumato* Algarotti praised in extravagant terms.

The differentiation between old and modern art, as we understand it today, was unknown to the age of rococo. In this respect Algarotti's vigorous plea for the formation of a collection of work by contemporary painters was all the more remarkable, especially as he advocated not only purchases, but direct commissions from the artists.

One of the finest works acquired as a result of this policy was Piazzetta's *Young Colour-bearer* (Gal. no. 571), bought by Algarotti in Venice in 1743. Two large purchases of Tiepolos were made in 1765, but these were unfortunately later resold.

Another important agent for the Dresden Gallery was the able and unscrupulous Ventura Rossi, who had been such a nuisance to Algarotti on his Italian trip. If we are to believe the allegations in the Count's letters – he must, of course, have been slightly prejudiced – Rossi managed to lay his hands on a number of works at little cost, and sold them later to the King at a considerable profit.

Rossi brought in many more pictures than his rival. In 1738 he sent a batch of 44 paintings to Dresden, followed in 1741 by 70 more; two years later came another 59, and in 1744 a further 67. One of his last purchases was the large *Christ in the Temple*, by Farinati (Gal. no. 223), from the Casa Bonfadini at Venice.

But comparatively few of his numerous contributions were of outstanding quality. Mention should be made of six landscapes by Marco Ricci (Gal. nos. 556–562) and of pictures by Guercino and

Bassano. Rossi also brought in a Spanish painting, *Christ healing the Blind Man*, by El Greco (Gal. no. 276), and two pictures by Ribera – *St Peter's Release from Prison* and *St Francis* (Gal. nos. 684, 685) – out of the Duodo collection at Venice. Rossi's chief merit lies in the part he played in the largest and most impressive transaction of the period, the purchase of the famous collection belonging to Duke Francesco III of Modena, for which the huge sum of 100,000 sequins was raised in 1745. The hundred pictures brought to Dresden from Modena in the following year, 1746, included the four large altarpieces by Correggio (Gal. nos. 150–153), the four magnificent paintings by Veronese which had come to Modena in 1645 from Venice, where the Cuccina family had previously owned them (Gal. nos. 224–227), Titian's famous *Tribute Money* (Gal. no. 169), his *Portrait of a Lady in White* and of his daughter *Lavinia* (Gal. nos. 170, 171), works by Andrea del Sarto, Giulio Romano and Tintoretto, and Parmigianino's icily shimmering *Madonna and Child with St Stephen and John the Baptist* (Gal. no. 160). The school of Ferrara was represented by allegorical paintings by Dossi, Girolamo da Carpi and Garofalo, which had hung in the Castle at Ferrara until 1618, when they were moved to Modena. Outstanding among the numerous seventeenth-century items are six splendid paintings by Annibale Carracci, some of them of large size, such as the picture of *St Roch* with its host of figures, and the grave *Madonna in Glory with St Matthew* (Gal. nos. 304, 305).

The *Portrait of the Sieur de Morette* by Hans Holbein the Younger (Gal. no. 1890) was then still ascribed to Leonardo da Vinci. Another incorrect, though not derogatory, attribution was made in the case of Velásquez's portrait of *Mateos* (Gal. no. 697), which was thought to be by Rubens. Rubens himself was represented by an early work, the life-sized *St Jerome* (Gal. no. 957). The purchase of the Modena collection gave Dresden the undisputed right to a place among the great European galleries. The fact that a transaction of such proportions and importance had been concluded was in itself enough to call forth astonishment and admiration on all sides.

However, this by no means exhausted the King's eagerness as a

42

buyer. Other Italian pictures brought to Dresden by various agents included—almost accidentally, it might seem—several valuable quattrocento works: two by Ercole Roberti (Gal. nos. 45, 46) from the sacristy of S. Giovanni at Bologna, and the wonderful *Annunciation* by Francesco Cossa (Gal. no. 43) from the Chiesa dell' Osservanza.

In 1747 Zanetti, the engraver, bought an early Titian, the *Santa Conversazione* (Gal. no. 168), from the Casa Grimani dei Servi at Venice, and other middlemen secured pictures by Franciabigio, Cignani and Reni. In 1752, Parmigianino's graceful *Madonna of the Rose* (Gal. no. 161) came to Dresden from the Casa Zani at Bologna.

Some projects unfortunately came to nothing. Negotiations were opened for Raphael's *Madonna di Foligno* and his *St Cecilia*, but without success; the best that Pietro Guarienti, Inspector of the Gallery (who from 1746 to 1753, kept the inventory which goes by his name) could achieve was to secure a copy of the latter work, by Dionysus Calvaert (Gal. no. 94). Domenichino's entrancing *Diana Bathing*, in the Villa Borghese, also eluded Dresden. This would have been a valuable addition to the impressive section of Bolognese seventeenth-century paintings, in which this artist is represented by only one picture, the *St Sebastian* (Gal. no. 319) purchased by Le Leu, the Paris agent, about 1750.

Other famous works with which Le Leu enriched the collection were Rembrandt's *Self-portrait with Saskia* (Gal. no. 1559) and Rubens' *Bathsheba* (Gal. no. 965), and he also acquired valuable pictures by Dou, Wouwerman and Teniers. Maratti's *Nativity* (Gal. no. 436) came to Dresden from Paris through his hands in 1744.

In Paris Augustus III had a second buyer for his Gallery, the Legation Secretary, de Brais. He sent in Rubens' *Mercury and Argus* (Gal. no. 962C), Vermeer's *Girl reading a Letter* (Gal. no. 1336), Rembrandt's *Saskia with a Red Rose* (Gal. no. 1562) and three works by Nicolas Poussin, *Adoration of the Magi, Moses in the Bullrushes,* and *Pan and Syrinx* (Gal. nos. 717, 720, 718).

Other complete collections were bought up, the most important being Count Wallenstein's from Dux, with its 268 pictures, for which 22,000 guilders was paid. This expense was justified by items such as

43

Vermeer's unique and magnificent *Procuress* (Gal. no. 1335) and two small portraits by Frans Hals (Gal. nos. 1358, 1359).

Several large groups of interesting pictures reached Dresden from the Imperial Gallery at Prague between 1742 and 1749, through the intermediary of Inspector Guarienti and Johann Gottfried Riedel (the latter had helped to arrange the earlier purchase of the Wallenstein collection). These included–to mention only a few of the most remarkable works acquired from this source–Rubens' *Boar Hunt* (Gal. no. 962), Honthorst's *Dentist* (Gal. no. 1251), *The Mystic Marriage of St Catherine* by Andrea del Sarto (Gal. no. 76), *The Cardsharper* by Valentin de Boulogne, which was at one time ascribed to Caravaggio (Gal. no. 408), and the fine series of pictures on biblical parables, by Fetti (Gal. nos. 410, 415–425).

The brilliant series of great acquisitions concluded with Raphael's *Sistine Madonna* (Gal. no. 93). It is curious that this particular work, previously little known, should later have become so famous that for many people it now epitomizes the Dresden Gallery. Its purchase was the outcome of more than a year's stubborn battling. On more than one occasion the representative of the Saxon Court, the Abbate Giovanni Battista Bianconi, advised Count Brühl to give up the idea and fall back on another Raphael, the *St Cecilia*, which could have been obtained much more easily and at less cost. But the King was determined to have the Madonna. He had very likely seen it at Piacenza in 1711, when he was a youth of fifteen making the Grand Tour and shortly to be converted to Catholicism, and thus the picture had intimate personal associations for him.

The Benedictines of the San Sisto Monastery, to whom the work belonged, were asking the rather formidable price of 36,000 scudi for it. In August 1752 Bianconi offered them 15,000 scudi, at first eliciting no response. In January 1753, however, the parties moved towards a compromise, the monks reducing their demand by 6,000 scudi and Bianconi raising his offer by 3,000. But this did not go far enough. Finally they agreed on 25,000 scudi. The negotiations were concluded in March 1753, and the price paid at once. Fresh difficulties arose at the last moment, however, when the Duke of Parma

44

refused to give an export permit, insisting on his sovereign right to prohibit the removal from his domains of a work of art which he considered to be of inestimable value—a completely modern attitude which, however, he was unable to maintain. But though the export permit was finally issued in September 1753, the removal of the picture was delayed until the beginning of 1754. At last, on 14th January 1754, Raphael's *Madonna* was carefully packed into a horsedrawn vehicle and sent on its way, reaching Dresden about a month later.

Julius Hübner, a later director of the Gallery, in his catalogue of its contents published in 1856, tells a story which, even if we doubt its authenticity, shows how highly the *Sistine Madonna* was valued at Dresden. 'King Augustus', he says, 'impatient to see again the picture he had so much longed to possess, ordered it to be unpacked at once and hung in the palace. Those who carried it into the throne-room were hesitating as to whether to place it in the best light, which was where the throne stood, when the King, with his own gracious hands, pushed the royal seat aside, saying "Make room for the great Raphael!" . . .'

A glance through the list of large consignments sent to Dresden in the first half of the eighteenth century reveals a remarkable soundness of judgment behind the transactions. Practically every group of purchases included masterpieces of the highest quality. This was by no means a matter of course, for in other places, such as Potsdam, unpleasant surprises were almost the order of the day when newly arrived pictures were unpacked. Severe disappointments were rare at Dresden. Only the Madrid agent, Legation Secretary Louis Talon, showed a tendency to bungle matters. In 1744 he sent a consignment of 125 pictures, most of which proved to be rubbish. The best of the worth-while pieces was Guercino's *Silvio and Dorinda* (Gal. no. 367). This brought down the wrath of Count Brühl on Talon's head. Brühl was the supreme authority. Since the accession of Augustus III he had been in control of all the royal art collections. Le Plat had nominally retained his post as Gallery director until his death in 1742, but his influence had been negligible, for the Prime Minister's authority was unchallenged in matters of art as in all others. Whether he had any real feeling for art, we cannot be sure. He could perhaps manage without, for his private secretary, Carl Heinrich von Heinecken (1706–1791) was a good and trustworthy adviser. Heinecken, born at Lübeck, where both his parents were artists, entered Brühl's service in 1739, soon took over the management of the picture gallery, and remained in this employment until after the Minister's death in 1763. He gave excellent service, not only in the Gallery itself but in the Cabinet of Engravings, which was his own creation.

Among the 'inspectors' who served with and after him were two who have already been mentioned – Johann Gottfried Riedel (1691–1755) and Pietro Guarienti (c. 1700–1753).

Half-way through the century, Heinecken enlisted a number of fine engravers and initiated an illustrated work about the Gallery, the *Recueil d'Estampes d'après les plus célèbres tableaux de la Galerie Royale de Dresde*, the first volume of which appeared in 1753; a second followed in 1754. Heinecken wrote descriptive notes for all the reproductions, and these, like his introduction, were printed in French. The foreword to the second volume contains, in addition to some theoretical observations on art, a brief history of the collection, which goes back as far as Elector Frederick the Wise and his association with Cranach.

Heinecken says that this work is meant for 'connoisseurs' and 'amateurs', in other words, for visitors to the Gallery, the fame of which it was intended to spread abroad. Except for Tobias Beutel's comparatively modest *Cedern-Wald* of 1671 it is the first evidence of any attempt at publicity. The choice of pictures for reproduction (each volume contains 50 plates) reflects the taste of the day. That Italian Renaissance and Baroque take foremost place is worth noting. This accords with the purchasing policy and general trend of the Gallery at that period, though Heinecken was quite aware that the chief wealth of the collection, which lay in its 'Flemish' (i.e. Dutch) pictures, was inadequately represented in his two volumes.

In a footnote to the second volume he refers with obvious pride to the Gallery's possession of 22 pictures by Teniers, 50 by Wouwerman, 21 by Dou, 15 by Mieris, 13 by Van der Werff, 9 by Netscher

46

and 12 by Berchem, saying that he thinks it appropriate to reproduce a landscape by the last of these as the final engraving in his series.

The few reproductions of works by Dutch masters include, at the end of the first volume, Rubens' large *Quos Ego*, depicting the triumphal arch erected at Antwerp for the Cardinal-Infante Ferdinand, which Count Brühl himself had acquired for the collection in 1742 (Gal. no. 964 B), and at the end of the second volume, Rembrandt's *Manoah's Offering* (Gal. no. 1563) and Van Dyck's *St Jerome* (Gal. no. 1024). Also in the second volume appears *Burgomaster Meyer's Madonna* by Holbein (Gal. no. 1892). Otherwise all the artists represented are Italian, except for Ribera, who has the great honour of seven reproductions. The early Renaissance Italian painters are also little represented; they include Cima's *Christ in Benediction* (Gal. no. 61), erroneously ascribed to Bellini, and Garofalo's *Athene and Poseidon* (Gal. no. 132), wrongly attributed to Francesco Francia, while the genuine Francia, *The Baptism of Christ* (Gal. no. 48) is missing. There are no examples of the work of contemporary artists. The emphasis is placed on Correggio, Titian, Veronese, Parmigianino, Tintoretto, Annibale Carracci, Reni, Fetti and, above all, Luca Giordano, ten of whose pictures are reproduced. Volume I opens with three of Correggio's works, while his *Holy Night* is the first reproduction in Volume II, thus testifying to the esteem in which this painter was held.

A surprising feature is Heinecken's omission of such famous paintings as Titian's *Tribute Money*, Giorgione's *Venus*, and, above all, Raphael's *Sistine Madonna*. This is partly explained in his introduction. He admits that the Gallery possesses '*deux Raphaels véritablement originaux*', but declares that there are other collections '*qui en ont en plus grand nombre*' and of greater beauty, as will be agreed by all '*qui ont examiné avec des yeux éclairés, à Versailles, la Ste Famille de Raphael*'; whereas in the 'divine' Corregio, Dresden possesses a treasure sufficient to compensate for any shortcomings in other respects. This assessment is born out by the chilly attitude towards Raphael's *Madonna* which Heinecken displays in his *Nachrichten von Künstlern und Kunstsachen*, published in 1769. But then, that

47

unique painting has been the subject of passionate controversy right up to our own day.

Heinecken's first volume of reproductions includes a ground-plan of the 'Stables', while the second volume includes an outside view. They are shown as built round a courtyard, and with a central wall running the whole length of the rooms. The inner gallery thus formed, overlooking the courtyard, contained the Italian pictures, while the Dutch, French and German works hung in the outer gallery. Behind the main galleries were two smaller rooms, one containing the collection's pastel pictures and the other for the use of painters – chiefly, no doubt, for copyists. Plan and elevation show the place as it was after the buildings in the 'stableyard' had been altered by Johann Christof Knöfel (1686–1752) between 1744 and 1746, large purchases

BERNARDO BELLOTTO (1720–1780) ▷
NEW MARKETPLACE, DRESDEN
Gallery No. 610, Canvas, 136×236 cm.

To the left of the picture we see the 'Stables' (built in the 1680's), in which the Dresden picture gallery was housed until 1855. Bellotto's picture shows the building as it was after being altered for the second time, in 1744–6. The valuable collection of pictures already called for better lighting – hence the large windows which lighten the façade and give it an almost classical aspect. The splendid double staircase had been added during the first alterations, in 1722–9.

Bellotto shows the square as larger than it was in reality. Above it towers the Frauenkirche, the most important basilica north of the Alps, with George Bähr's massive yet slender dome. The exaggerated perspective must be laid to the blame of the *camera obscura*, of which Bellotto made use for many of his architectural pictures. The lenses of that day allowed little light to pass through, so that the apparatus was useless except in strong sunlight. This accounts for the bright light with which Bellotto's pictures are uniformly flooded, and their lack of depth. The most distant objects stand out sharply, as though a stone's throw away, instead of being wrapped in the poetic mist of which uncle, Canaletto, was so fond.

King August III's coach drawn by six horses comes dashing across the market-place. It was no mere chance that the artist paid a compliment to his patron on this particular spot, for Augustus III took special pride in his picture gallery which was already famous.

Bellotto delivered this picture direct to the Gallery, in 1751.

48

having for the second time reduced the collection to an intolerably cramped condition. The lighting had been improved by cutting large windows, topped by semicircular blind arches, and the projecting structures at the corners had been demolished. Inside, the first floor and the attic storey had been made into one, so that the galleries were high-ceilinged and well lit.

While rebuilding was in progress, the pictures were kept in the Japanese Palace. The operation was completed in 1747, and the valuable paintings from the Modena collection arrived at exactly the right moment to benefit from it.

We have no detailed information as to how the pictures were arranged. To judge by contemporary views of other interiors, they must have covered the walls as far up as the cornice, hanging in serried ranks, with the smaller works below and the larger ones above. They were all in rococo frames, specially prepared by Deibel and Kugler, the Gallery's woodcarvers, for the new premises. They have remained in those frames until the present day, which is one of the principal reasons for the impression of unity so much praised by visitors to the Dresden Gallery. The general effect must have been most imposing and magnificent, in the true spirit of Baroque, with a rich and lavish quality recalling the old-time 'treasury'. Even after this rebuilding, however, the place was not exactly what contemporaries expected a 'Gallery' to be. Thomas Nugent, an English traveller, remarks upon this in his book, *The Grand Tour*, published in London in 1756. He compares the royal collection with Brühl's private gallery, and notes with surprise that the latter, though a good deal smaller, produces a finer general effect and is, indeed, 156 ells in length, or longer by 18 ells than the *Galerie des glaces* at Versailles. He gives special praise to the arrangement of the pictures, which received the full light from the row of windows in the opposite wall, and points out that the mirrors placed between the pillars help to enhance the general impression.

This example shows that the general appearance of the room, the harmony established between its architecture and its decoration, was of paramount importance in an art gallery of this period. Individual paintings, however much they might be admired, were little more than decorative elements contributing to that effect. If a connoisseur wished to inspect an individual picture more closely, it had to be taken down a placed on an easel; there was no difficulty about this, for the collection was not yet open to the general public.

But the Gallery's great phase was now drawing to close. There were no really important acquisitions in the second half of the century, after the purchase of the *Sistine Madonna*. All such activities were brought to an end by the Seven Years War, which broke out in 1756. Augustus III died in 1763, and Brühl shortly afterwards. Heinecken was brought to trial. In a memorandum dated 1st December 1763 he replies to the charges brought against him and asks what crimes he has committed. 'The grounds (of the accusation) cannot', he says, 'be found in the allegations made to me by an estimable Commission, concerning the emptiness of the coffers and the burden of debt. For I have made it too clear that I never had anything to do with the royal coffers. It is true that when I saw and heard of the vast sums being laid out on all sides, it was plain to me, as a man of good sense, that the revenues of the Electorate of Saxony must be insufficient to produce them. But I am not to blame for that expenditure, nor did I give order for even the least part of it.'

Heinecken was acquitted. It was Brühl who should really have been in the dock, for it was his mismanagement which had resulted in the total collapse of the national economy, for which the whole population now had to pay the penalty. A new, bourgeois period lay ahead, confronting even the Gallery with new tasks.

INTERLUDE

The period–barely a century–between the outbreak of the Seven Years War and the transfer of the Gallery to Gottfried Semper's new museum building in the Zwinger, constituted a pause during which the collection lived on the fame of its glorious past, undergoing no appreciable changes. Important purchases were out of the question until half way through the nineteenth century, after the havoc wrought in the national finances by Count Brühl's irresponsible policies.

It is typical of the mentality of Augustus III, however that in 1763, immediately after the fiasco of the Seven Years War, he had attempted to begin collecting again as though nothing had happened, and had opened negotiations at The Hague for the purchase of pictures from the Lormier collection. His death brought this plan to nothing, and the agreements already concluded were cancelled. The only one of the works under consideration to reach Dresden was Rembrandt's *The Entombment* (Gal. no. 1566), a copy, made in the master's studio and finished by his own hand, of the original in Munich. The purchase in the following year, 1764, of Guido Reni's *Virgin with the sleeping Child* (Gal. no. 326) was the last transaction until the end of the century. Even the work of living artists, though much less costly, was disregarded, with the exception of three fine paintings by Goethe's friend Angelica Kauffmann (Gal. nos. 2181–2183), bought in 1782.

Other additions, such as the 87 paintings seized in 1778 from the estate of the late Senior Auditor Spahn as compensation for money he had embezzled, were of so little value as to be more in the nature of an embarrassment to the overcrowded Gallery. And while gains were negligible, losses were palpable.

In 1760 the Prussian troops had sacked the castle of Hubertusburg, near Oschatz, and many of the pictures stored there had disappeared. Other items were sold by auction. The surviving works from Huber-

51

tusburg came under the hammer at Amsterdam in 1765, including Tiepolo's large *Antony and Cleopatra*, bought by Algarotti at Venice in 1743. In 1796 another auction took place, comprising what were described as duplicates. As this produced no more than 679 thalers, however, the idea of further auctions was given up. In 1769 there was another sale, at which Carl Heinrich von Heinecken, who since his dismissal from office had been earning his living as a writer on art, bought 132 pictures from the Gallery, most of them by early German painters, for the sum of 7,900 thalers.

The Seven Years War not only put a stop to purchases for the Dresden Gallery, but brought all kinds of dangers to the existing collection. When the Prussian army entered Saxony, Augustus III and Count Brühl immediately took refuge in the fortress of Königstein, near Dresden, and in October 1756, when the Saxon troops capitulated, they continued their flight as far as Warsaw. Only Queen Maria Josepha and the heir to the throne remained at Dresden.

The entire responsibility for the precious collection of pictures rested with Johann Anton Riedel (1733–1816) who, on the death of his father, Johann Gottfried, in 1755, had become one of the two Gallery Inspectors–the other being Matthias Oesterreich, a cousin of Heinecken's. In 1757 Oesterreich retired, and Riedel became sole head of the Gallery.

On 7th September 1756 the 'Stables' were locked up and the key given to the Queen, to whom Frederick the Great had to apply for permission to view. Frederick paid several lengthy visits to the famous collection, which may prompted him to a certain envy. Riedel notes in his journal on 18th September that 'the King of Prussia came to the Gallery at 10 o'clock this morning, accompanied only by Prince Henry, all the servants of the Gallery being required to absent themselves during his visit, and remained until 12 o'clock.' When the Queen died, in 1757, the Crown Prince took charge of the key.

In view of the various dangers resulting from the war, Riedel felt it wise to take precautions. In August 1758, for example, the pictures stored in the Japanese Palace were hastily loaded into carts and moved away, for fear the approach of the Austrian army might

52

cause the Prussians to set fire to the neighbouring powder magazine. Although Dresden suffered considerably during the hostilities, no appreciable damage was done to the Gallery premises. Not until the Prussian garrison surrendered to the Austrian army on 4th September 1759, was Riedel ordered to pack up the paintings and send them – in three shiploads – to the fortress of Königstein on the Elbe. Even so the 'Stables' were not completely emptied, for Riedel's report states that 'the pictures are still hanging on the pillars'!

The atmospheric conditions in the new storage premises were not of the best. 'The pictures in the Fortress were inspected two or three times per month, those on rollers being unrolled and dusted each spring and autumn, this being continued until they were taken back again.' An order for their return was given at the beginning of July 1760, owing to increasing evidence of their being affected by damp. The pastels, the pride of the Gallery, which were particularly sensitive, had already been taken back to Dresden. Packing of the remaining pictures had no sooner begun than the order was countermanded, as the Prussian army was moving back towards Dresden.

Riedel's care for the treasures entrusted to him was beyond praise. 'On the morning of the 12th July (1760)', he writes in his journal, 'the Prussians marched on Dresden, the city being already surrounded by 5 o'clock that evening; on the morning of the 13th at 6 o'clock the bombardment began (. . . I had water brought up at once, to supplement the 4 buckets of water which stood in the Gallery in case of emergency) by the battery outside the Pirnau Gate, when the first shells fell in the Gallery, though with no harm done except that the window of the Pastel Cabinet was badly damaged and all the glass in the windows was broken, the firing continued until almost eleven in the morning, when the battery was demolished, and many shells of 6 and even of 8 tt fell in the Gallery, one of which caused a fire, the windows of the Gallery were much damaged through the bursting of the shells thus falling inside.' Francesco Francia's *Baptism of Christ* had been damaged 'to left, on the tree', by a piece of shrapnel. Riedel thought it advisable to have a number of pictures 'some of which being under repair and others left here because of the great

53

dampness of the Fortress, to be packed and with all documents and records, and an inventory', conveyed 'in a boat to Koenigstein.'

The town had suffered badly in the bombardment. A picture by Bernardo Bellotto shows the suburb of Pirnau in ruins, and the shattered Church of the Holy Cross appears in another of his paintings (Gal. no. 638), its broken tower rising from a heap of rubble like a silent indictment of war. This view was painted in 1765, when rebuilding had just begun.

It took a long time to efface all evidence of destruction. When Goethe, then a nineteen-year-old student, arrived on a visit from Leipzig in 1768, five years after the end of the war, many parts of the town still lay in ruins. In the eighth book of *Dichtung und Wahrheit* he records his impressions, and admits that his enthusiasm for art was 'interrupted and damped by the most melancholy prospects', owing to 'the damaged and desolate condition of so many of the streets of Dresden through which I walked. The ruins of the Mohrenstraße, and the Kreuzkirche with its shattered tower, made a deep impression on me and still remain like a dark patch in my mind's eye. I looked down from the dome of the Frauenkirche on these grievous ruins scattered about the beautifully ordered city, while the verger praised the skill of the architect who had already rebuilt church and dome after this lamentable event, strengthening them against bombs. The worthy sacristan then pointed to the surrounding ruins and said tersely, "That was done by the enemy!"'

When Goethe visited Dresden the Gallery was in order again. A month after peace was signed at Hubertusburg (March 1763) the pictures were brought back to the 'Stables' from the fortress of Königstein. They seem to have suffered less during their absence than might be expected from Riedel's report. Dassdorf, in his *Beschreibung der vorzüglichsten Merkwürdigkeiten in der Churfürstlichen Residenzstadt Dresden*, published in 1782, could still give warm praise to the excellent condition of the paintings. Goethe was much impressed by his visit to the Gallery. 'My admiration exceeded anything that I had expected', he writes. 'This Gallery, now returning to itself, in which magnificence and good order prevailed amid the deepest

54

silence, the gleaming frames, still fresh as when they were first gilded, the polished floor, the great halls paced by visitors rather than used by workers, gave a unique feeling of solemnity, the more akin to that with which one enters a church, in that the treasures of many chapels, the objects of so much reverence, are here displayed anew in the sacred cause of art.'

For the young poet, as for many other visitors to Dresden, the Gallery and its treasures were the town's chief attraction. Even the famous antiques left him cold; he 'refused to see them, or any of the other precious things in Dresden.' This is all the more astonishing because Winckelmann's *Gedanken über die Nachahmung der griechischen Werke in der Malerey und Bildhauerkunst (Thoughts on the Imitation of Greek Works in Painting and Sculpture)* had been the gospel of many leading intellectuals since it was first published in the year 1755.

On this first visit to the Gallery Goethe made the acquaintance of Inspector Riedel, whom he describes as 'an excellent man, as active and obliging at that time as I found him to be several years thereafter, and as he still shows himself today.' Shortly before his return to Leipzig he was introduced to Christian Ludwig von Hagedorn, who showed him over his collection 'with much kindness, and took the greatest delight in the enthusiasm of the young art-lover.'

Hagedorn (1712–1780), who succeeded Heinecken in 1764, was, like his predecessor, a writer on art and had published his own *Betrachtungen über die Malerey* in 1762. A new type of museum specialist was now coming to the fore, one who did not rest content with technical occupations, but tackled theoretical problems as well. Le Plat and those like him had brought a somewhat amateur approach to their practical tasks. But in the intellectual atmosphere of the Enlightenment, the aristocratic dilettante began to feel himself called upon to give a written account of his ideas and actions. Algarotti had already attempted something of the kind.

This gave fresh impetus to aesthetic theories, according with the view that art had something to teach and was itself a subject for study. The new movement took its lead from Johann Joachim Winckelmann

55

(1717–1768), who had himself worked at Dresden from 1748 to 1754. Many Academies of Art came into being as a result. One of these was founded at Dresden in 1764, with Hagedorn as its first Director. This meant that one man was at the head of two institutions originally intended to serve completely different purposes, and the repercussions were felt by the Gallery. It ceased to be purely a private royal collection, serving to enhance the ruler's prestige and reflecting his views on art. It began to influence taste, to reveal an objective aspect coupled with a claim to public attention. Anton Raphael Mengs, who had been Court painter at Dresden since 1745 and was among the most admired artists of the classical movement, regarded the Gallery as first and foremost the noble school in which he had learnt his art. The situation was not unlike that in fifteenth-century Florence, when Lorenzo de' Medici opened the gardens of San Marco to painters and sculptors for purposes of study.

But it was not only artists who demanded admission to the Gallery. The general public also began to reveal an urge for a more democratic policy. In this connection the most far-reaching event was the decree promulgated by the French National Convention in 1793, by which the royal art collections became national property and the Louvre Museum was opened to the public.

Things went more slowly at Dresden. In the early decades of the nineteenth century it was still difficult to obtain permission to visit the Gallery, and even prominent people sometimes had reason to complain. In many cases Inspectors required a sizeable tip, just as in the time of Tobias Beutel, in return for a permit.

The situation remained the same until the publication of the Constitution of 4th September 1831, which transferred the Gallery to State ownership. Thereupon, Minister of State Lindenau, who had been Director-General of Art Collections since 1830, announced that from August 'until the end of October of the present year, with the exception of Sundays and public holidays', the Gallery would be 'open daily from 9 a.m. to 1 p.m. to respectably dressed persons.' This regulation could obviously benefit only those who were in a position to do as they wished with their time, even on weekdays.

56

The management of the royal properties had already been transferred to the State on a previous occasion – after the Battle of Leipzig, when Frederick Augustus I (1750–1827) had been taken prisoner and the authority had passed into the hands of the Russian Governor, Prince Nikolas Repnin-Volkonsky. During the Napoleonic Wars, as previously in the Seven Years War, part of the collection of paintings had been removed to Königstein for safety. During his period of office (12th October 1813 to 8th November 1814), Repnin tried to hasten the return of the pictures, as he wanted to make them accessible to the public. In this he failed completely. The works concerned were brought back after Frederick Augustus was released from imprisonment (1815), and restored to the ownership of the royal family, so that everything was as before.

Evidence that museums were confronted by new tasks when democracy began to take root is provided by the fact that now they not only kept inventories, but produced catalogues for the benefit of visitors. In the years 1804–1809, Inspector Riedel prepared a new General Inventory as a follow-up to the *'Inventarium'* made by Matthias Oesterreich in 1754, which listed 1,446 pictures. Prior to this, however, in 1765, he had brought out the first catalogue in the French language, followed in 1771 by a German version. The pictures were listed in the order in which they were hung, and a short biographical note was appended to the accompanying description. It is clear from the Introduction to this catalogue that the Gallery was regarded as a school for forming the nation's taste, an attitude which was quite in the spirit of Raphael Mengs and the classicists.

At that time 1,344 paintings, not including pastels, were on display in the 'Stables'. Further catalogues were published in 1812, 1817, 1818 and 1822. These were edited by the painter Carl Frederick Demiani (1768–1823), who succeeded Anton Riedel as Inspector in the year 1816. A new publication, *Die vorzüglichsten Gemälde der Königlichen Galerie in Dresden nach den Originalen auf Stein gezeichnet*, containing 185 reproductions and a descriptive text, was issued by Hanfstaengl at Dresden in 1836. It is a sign of the times that the new and inexpensive process of lithography was used for this volume.

The costly and aristocratic etchings used by Heinecken in 1753 to illustrate his selection of pictures belonged to the distant past.

It is clear from the catalogues and inventories of this period that though buying was practically at a standstill, acquisitions were being made in various other ways. Pictures found in castles, churches and other buildings were sometimes brought to the Gallery. In 1817, for example, a number of Dutch seventeenth-century paintings arrived; these had at one time hung in the private apartments of Augustus III, and had since then spent fifty-four years hidden away in packing-cases. In 1834, after a number of other additions had been made, Von Lindenau ordered a general inspection of the collection.

It became increasingly evident that in the interests of visitors the pictures should be rearranged. An attempt to give them more light and space, in accordance with the tastes of the classicists, had already succeeded in Berlin and Munich, but it failed at Dresden for lack of suitable premises.

The Baroque exuberance of the Dresden Gallery, in particular, made an unfavourable impression, as is apparent from the description by the philosopher Heinrich Steffens (1773–1845), who visited the collection as a young man at the turn of the century. While astonished at first by the unexpected number of celebrated paintings, Steffens goes on to say: 'The motley colours seemed to dance before my eyes, and the painters' names whirled in an equal confusion, for though some of them were familiar to me already, I was hearing the greater number for the first time.' The pictures did not yet bear labels, such as are taken for granted everywhere nowadays; those were not provided until the 1830's. 'Feeling terribly sleepy and tired,' continues Steffens, 'I tried hard to pull myself together, but it was no use ... Meanwhile, the monotonous tones of the guide, supplying information I was expected to assimilate, rang strangely in my ears ... The tour of the Gallery was now almost finished, and I thanked heaven when we were out of doors again.'

Steffens is honest enough to admit that his confusion did not result solely from the congestion in the Gallery; but his report shows how bewildering the place must have seemed to an unprepared visitor.

58

The only improvement to result from the general inspection in 1834 was that partitions were set up on which pictures could be hung, compensating in some degree for the lack of space. At this time, too, the pictures, which until then had been arranged chiefly according to size, were brought into something resembling systematic order, which made it easier to obtain a general view of them.

But only a new building could solve the problem of space, and this had in fact been under consideration since 1836. It was, however, the question of looking after the pictures which finally decided the matter. The condition they were in had brought complaints as early as the 1820's. Not until then does the damage suffered during their various removals seem to have become gradually apparent. In 1823 Demiani was succeeded by Johann Friedrich Matthäi (1777–1845), a professor at the Dresden Academy of Art. Matthäi had a trained eye for the technical problems of painting, and began to ponder the care and restoration of the pictures in his charge. There were no really experienced picture restorers at Dresden in those days. When such work was needed, it had so far been entrusted to one or other of the Court painters. Bottschild has already been mentioned in the history of the *Kunstkammer* and – to mention only one other name – some restoration had been done at a later period by Christian Wilhelm Dietrich (who was appointed as Court painter in 1741, rose to be Gallery Inspector in 1746, and taught at the Dresden Academy of Art from 1765 onwards).

To secure the services of a recognized expert, the Gallery authorities sent to Rome in 1826 for an Italian, Pietro Palmaroli (c. 1778–1828), who dealt with several Dutch paintings and fifty-four Italian works, including Titian's *Tribute Money* and *Lady in White*, Correggio's *Holy Night* and Veronese's large picture, *The Madonna with the Cuccina family*. His experience was helpful to Inspector Johann August Renner (born 1783, still living in 1869) and later to Martin Schirmer (1808–1876), enabling them to improve their own work considerably.

Renner used to stick small labels on the back of the pictures he handled, giving brief particulars of the restoration carried out. In

59

1836 a 'Gallery Committee' was set up; with the exception of Matthäi, the Director, and representatives of the Government, its members were all painters. The ascendancy of artists is a characteristic feature of museum organization in the middle of the nineteenth century. This group concentrated on the discussion of problems connected with the care of pictures. A report dated 28th February 1837 lists 950 paintings as being in need of cleaning, varnishing or restoration. Their bad state of preservation was attributed to the lack of facilities in the 'Stables'. There was no heating there, so that abrupt changes of temperature occurred from one season to the next. The paintings on wood suffered worst of all from this. Moreover, 'coal-fumes' settled on the pictures and darkened the varnish. For these reasons, if for no others, the Committee was strongly in favour of a new building.

The first idea was to turn the Zwinger into a museum. Fortunately this plan was not carried out, for the necessary alterations (the existing buildings were to be extended, and further storeys added) would have completely destroyed the unique quality of an architectural monument, the beauty of which was entirely lost on the people of that period.

Meanwhile, Gottfried Semper had been commissioned to draw up plans for a new building. The first designs were submitted on 8th April 1838. A new chapter in the history of the Gallery was about to begin.

60

THE GALLERY IN SEMPER'S BUILDING

Gottfried Semper (1803–79) was invited to Dresden in 1834 to teach at the Academy of Art and to become head of the School of Architecture. He was proposed for these duties by Friedrich Schinkel, to whom the post had first been offered.

Schinkel had designed the Old Museum in Berlin (1822–28), a building which owed its origin to a new, romantic outlook. Winckelmann and the classicists had tried to make public art collections into educational institutions where the nation's taste could be trained; in the early nineteenth century, museums began to be regarded as shrines of aestheticism. This made specific demands on the buildings themselves, and architects had to take such demands into account.

Schinkel consequently took the Pantheon in Rome as the model for his Berlin Museum, designing a central hall, surmounted by a dome, as the holy of holies where the finest works in the collection were to hang. This would put an unprepared visitor, as soon as he entered the building, into the serious, uplifted frame of mind which the Romantics considered essential for any fruitful contact with art.

The private royal collections of the eighteenth century had not followed these architectural principles, for in them the individual work of art had been merely one decorative element of an ensemble, not an object for separate display.

The public museum of the nineteenth century was a different matter. It had to satisfy practical as well as ideal requirements, for its contents, if they were to be made accessible to visitors, required systematic arrangement which was only possible in suitably designed premises. The first large building to meet these demands in a really satisfactory manner was the Alte Pinakothek, built in Munich (1826–30) to the designs of Leo von Klenze.

Klenze rejected the idea of the 'holy of holies', and was thus able to dispense with the domed hall which was never satisfactory from

61

the point of view of lighting, though regarded in the Berlin Museum as necessary on ideological grounds. Klenze thought it more important to present the pictures as favourably as possible. The result was a type of building which, with its succession of galleries well lit from above and its parallel row of smaller rooms, was to serve as the pattern for many later museums, among them the new Dresden Gallery.

From 1838 onwards, Gottfried Semper drew up a number of plans for different sites. These all came to nothing because in 1840 the Diet refused to vote the necessary appropriation, declaring that most of the projects would be too costly. The site at the open end of the Zwinger was still considered to be the best.

The Gallery Commission, as the 'Galerie Comité' of 1836 was now called, declared itself, after careful scrutiny of all the plans, to be in favour of a building which would form a link between the 'German' and 'French' pavilions of the Zwinger. The Commission's report states that 'The model proposed would make the Museum the principal building of the Zwinger, not only because its actual size would dominate its surroundings, but because of its noble and solemn style. The neighbouring arcades and pavilions would have the aspect of cheerful, festive decorations for the more dignified palace of art.'

This opinion illustrates the values of the classical period, which had no appreciation of Baroque as a medium of expression. An article written in 1856 also mentions the problem of 'combining the Gallery harmoniously' with the 'rich though turgid rococo style of the Zwinger'.

This did indeed present difficulties which only an architect of great sensitivity could solve. It was not, as was then supposed, a matter of inducing old-fashioned 'turgid' buildings to tone in with the 'noble solemnity' of a loftier style, but of combining two basically incompatible concepts of form. The lapse of time is now beginning to show the much-decried architecture of the nineteenth century in a more favourable light, and helps the present-day observer to concede that Semper handled the problem successfully.

It may seem curious that his design reverts to the romantic idea of the 'holy of holies', already abandoned by Klenze for practical rea-

62

sons. But the site of the building may have forced him to do so, for in order to balance the Kronentor on the far side of the Zwinger courtyard, the new gallery also had to have a central arch and a dome. An octagonal hall in the middle of the building thus seemed the obvious solution. This Rotunda, as it was called, was bound to be unsuitable for the display of pictures, as only a dim light filtered through the high windows surrounding the dome. Furthermore, the sequence of the large exhibition rooms on the first floor was broken because the one immediately above the arched entrance on the ground floor had to be on an appreciably higher level than those to either side of it.

While building was actually in progress, the height of the dome was reduced in order to afford better lighting conditions. This did not improve the outer aspect of the building, but aesthetic considerations had to give way to the technical requirements of the exhibition it was to contain.

Semper had no further say in these measures, for as a result of taking part in the uprising of May 1849 he had been obliged to leave Dresden before the building was finished. In an open letter sent from Paris in 1852, he protested against the changes made in his original plan. Seen from the Theaterplatz, the Gallery has the appearance of a monumental, massive construction in the Italian style of the late Renaissance. From the central courtyard of the Zwinger, on which side the second floor is set back a little, it has a less heavy appearance, reasonably in keeping with graceful, relaxed style of Daniel Pöppelmann.

The central arch divides the ground floor of Semper's building into two unconnected sections. To the east lay a gallery, divided by pillars into three aisles, which was to hold the Mengs collection of plaster casts. This had been arranged on the ground floor of the 'Stables' since 1794. The corresponding gallery on the opposite side of the arch gave access to the picture gallery itself, by way of the Cabinet of Engravings. Beyond the latter came a magnificent staircase leading to the main exhibition rooms on the first floor. The Rotunda was flanked to either side by three rooms lit by windows placed high up,

63

and bordered on the north and south by a series of small cabinets; behind the Rotunda, two comparatively narrow stairways led to the second floor, with its suite of smaller rooms with lower ceilings, also lit from above.

The foundation stone of the new gallery was laid on 23rd July 1848. The foundations themselves were still being dug when doubts arose as to whether the building would not prove to be too small to house the entire collection of existing pictures. It was therefore decided to alter the original plan by carrying the two ends of the building up to the level of the main roof, thus gaining extra space on the second-floor level on either side. After Semper's flight, in May

BERNARDO BELLOTTO (1720–1780)   ▷
THE ZWINGER, DRESDEN
Gallery No. 629, Canvas, 134×238 cm.

The Zwinger buildings are like a bright garland surrounding a spacious ballroom open to the sky.

Daniel Pöppelmann's designs for this most remarkable of all Baroque projects were carried out, at the order of Augustus the Strong, in several stages, from 1710 onwards. It was originally to have been simply an Orangerie, composed of graceful pavilions linked by arches and richly decorated with carving; but it gradually took firmer shape. It takes its name from the site beside the Elbe, across which the fortified city wall had once run.

Bellotto's picture shows the Zwinger in the drab light of common day. The period of uproarious fancy dress balls, when money was heedlessly squandered on illuminations and fireworks, had already come to an end. Indeed, the Zwinger was never even completed. The north side of the courtyard was left open, for after the disastrous conclusion of the Seven Years War there was no money to carry out the remainder of Pöppelmann's richly imaginative designs, which are known to us only through an album of engravings. With the change of taste that took place in the latter half of the eighteenth century, initiated by the writings of Winckelmann, Baroque came to be regarded by the classicists as a confused, exaggerated and tasteless art form, and the buildings were left to sink into gradual decay. Not until the middle of the nineteenth century was the fourth side of the courtyard filled, by Gottfried Semper's gallery, where the Dresden collection of pictures has been housed ever since its removal from the 'Stables' in 1855.

This picture appears for the first time in the inventory of the Gallery's contents made in 1754.

64

1849, building operations were suspended for a short time. After that Krüger, the Court architect, and the *Landbaumeister*, Haenel, divided the responsibility between them. Haenel made several visits to Berlin and Munich, to study the interior arrangement of their museums from the technical angle. His most important innovation was the installation of a hot air plant to heat the ground floor, with a hot water system for the upper floors. In 1840, long before building was actually started, Von Lindenau had sent a representative to Belgium, Holland, England and France, to inspect museums and decide which of their features could be applied to Dresden.

The gallery took seven years to build, and the opening ceremony was held on 25th September 1855. During the transfer of pictures from the 'Stables', which had begun on 31st May of that year, 'not one of the 2,200 pictures had been damaged'. They covered the entire display surface of the walls, hanging in three or four rows from the top of the wainscoting right up to the cornice. A historical grouping according to schools was undertaken on a large scale for the first time, but in most respects the situation was much the same as it had been in the 'Stables' and the impression of overcrowding still persisted, though the serried ranks of valuable pictures must have been a rather imposing sight.

The conception of the art gallery as a 'holy of holies' was recalled only in the treatment accorded the *Sistine Madonna*. The first idea had been to hang that famous painting in the Rotunda, together with the four altarpieces by Correggio, but this had been abandoned owing to the bad lighting conditions. After that no-one knew what to do with the Rotunda. At last, for want of a better scheme, it was decided to fall back on the 'Raphael tapestries' – the seventeenth-century English copies of the originals in the Vatican. The *Sistine Madonna* was then put by itself in a chapel-like room at the far end of the west wing, which thus became something in the nature of a 'shrine'.

Despite the careful consideration given to the plans for the new building, certain defects came to light after the pictures were installed. No arrangements had been made for reserves, storerooms or workshops, or for the seven hundred pictures known as 'duplicates'.

65

These last had to be left for the time being in what was once Count Brühl's private gallery. Some of them, the 'third choice', were put up for auction at Dresden between 1859 and 1861, producing the modest sum of 8,440 thalers. The remainder were distributed among the royal castles—with the exception of the best pieces, which were placed in the Gallery, after which not an inch of free space remained. Moreover, the plans had taken no account of the natural tendency to growth which characterizes every collection. This had been forgotten because practically no purchases had been made for a hundred years, Dresden having let slip all the opportunities of which Berlin and Munich had taken such magnificent advantage. Owing to this lack of official initiative the early German, Dutch and Italian work, whose demure charm had been discovered by the Romantics, is very poorly represented in the Gallery.

On the other hand, the purchasing hiatus had the advantage of leaving the early eighteenth-century atmosphere of the Dresden Gallery almost unimpaired.

In the middle of the nineteenth century, even before Semper's building came into use, there were signs of a renewed interest in buying. The year 1852 was marked by the acquisition of an important work by a contemporary of Dürer, the *St Ursula* triptych by Jorg Breu the Elder (Gal. no. 1888). A year later, fifteen paintings by Spanish masters were bought in London for the sum of £579, making a most welcome addition to the Gallery's small existing group of Spanish works. These came from the collection of Louis-Philippe, the 'Roi bourgeois', who fled to England after the Paris revolution of February 1848, and died there two years later. The principal items were Zurbarán's *St Bonaventure* (Gal. no. 696), Murillo's *St Rodriguez* (Gal. no. 704) and works by Orrente (Gal. no. 677), Juan de Valdés Leal (Gal. no. 707) and Pereyra (Gal. no. 675). Another large Murillo was added in 1894, the *Death of St Clara* (Gal. no. 703 B), which also came from England, from the Earl of Dudley's collection.

The purchase had been arranged by Ludwig Gruner, the curator of the Cabinet of Engravings, thanks to whom other important works were acquired during these decades, chiefly in London, to fill gaps in

66

the collection. Most of these were quattrocento pictures, to which Dresden had hitherto paid little attention. In 1860 two pictures were bought from the heirs of the London art-dealer Woodburne–a small *Madonna and the Infant John the Baptist* by Lorenzo di Credi (Gal. no. 13) and the *Tondo: Holy Family and Angels* by Piero di Cosimo (Gal. no. 20). Both of them, however, were wrongly ascribed, the Credi being sold as a Leonardo and the Piero di Cosimo as a Signorelli. In 1874 two more pictures by Credi arrived from London, bought from the Barker collection (Gal. nos. 14, 15).

As an example of the splendid opportunities neglected by the Gallery, it may be mentioned that the purchases made from the Barker collection by the National Gallery in London included such masterpieces as the *Birth of Christ with the singing angels*, by Piero della Francesca (no. 908) and *Venus with the sleeping Mars*, by Botticelli (no. 915).

Nevertheless even Dresden had some strokes of luck. In 1868, for instance, a fine example of Botticelli's later work, *Four Scenes from the Life of St Zenobius* (Gal. no. 9) was acquired from the Quandt collection. But the most important new purchases were made for the quattrocento section, with *The Martyrdom of St Sebastian*, by Antonello da Messina (Gal. no. 52), bought at Vienna in 1873, and *The Holy Family* by Mantegna (Gal. no. 51), bought in London in 1876, through the good offices of Ludwig Gruner, from the heirs of Sir Charles Eastlake. The last addition to this early Italian group was made in 1922, with the purchase of the *Madonna Reading*, by Lorenzo Costa (Gal. no. 47 A).

An unfortunate gap in the ranks of the eighteenth-century Italian painters was closed, too, when the *Vision of St Anne*, by Giovanni Battista Tiepolo (Gal. no. 580 A) was bought from a Paris dealer in 1926, followed in 1927 by the purchase from a Berlin dealer of the same master's *Triumph of Amphitrite* (Gal. no. 580 B). Funds for the latter being insufficient, it was exchanged for some of the Gallery's 'duplicates' (by Mieris the Elder, Hobbema and Wouwerman).

Additions to the Dutch and Flemish section included Heda's *Breakfast Table with Blackberry Pie* (Gal. no. 1371), bought in 1875 from

67

an Antwerp dealer, Jan Steen's *Dismissal of Hagar* (Gal. no. 1727), purchased from the Dresden dealer Ernst in 1876, and *Two Horsemen*, by Thomas de Keyser (Gal. no. 1543), bought from a Viennese dealer in 1880. In 1899 came Hobbema's *Watermill* (Gal. no. 1664 A) and in 1905, from a London dealer, the fine *Landscape with Sand-dunes* by Philips Koninck (Gal. no. 1612 A), which compensated to some extent for the absence of any example of Rembrandt's landscape painting in the Dresden Gallery. A last fine example of Dutch painting—*Street in Haarlem*, by Gerrit Berckheyde (Gal. no. 1523 A)—was acquired in 1912, when the Weber collection came up for auction in Hamburg.

The earliest Flemish and German art had always been virtually ignored, and no attempt to remedy this was made until the beginning of the twentieth century. In 1903 a characteristic specimen of German late Gothic painting was purchased—the *Lamentation over the Dead Christ* by the Master of the Hausbuch, (Gal. no. 1868 A). Lucas Cranach and his school were particularly popular. In 1905, two portraits by him *(Duke Henry the Pious and his wife, Katherine of Mecklenburg*, Gal. no. 1906 H), known to have been in the *Kunstkammer* since 1641, were transferred to the Gallery from the History Museum. In 1917 a small *Birth of Christ* was bought at the sale of the Kaufmann collection in Berlin (Gal. no. 1907 A), and in 1928 *The Garden of Eden* (Gal. no. 2908 A) was acquired. A magnificent addition was made to the Cranach collection in 1929—the two side panels of the Schneeberg altarpiece *(Christ on the Mount of Olives* with the portrait of *Johann Friedrich the Magnanimous*, and the *Resurrection* with the portrait of *Duke Johann Ernst of Saxony*, Gal. nos. 1915 A and B). The year 1927 saw the purchase of *Mucius Scaevola* by Hans Baldung, known as Grien (Gal. no. 1888 B).

The section of eighteenth-century German art was enriched by a number of gifts, including several portraits by Anton Graff. A large painting by Fuseli representing a scene from *A Midsummer Night's Dream* came from Zürich in 1927 (Gal. no. 798 E). *Hercules at the Crossroads*, by Johann Liss (Gal. no. 1841 A) was bought in England in 1925.

68

From the latter half of the nineteenth century on, purchases had been directed towards contemporary art, but particulars of the works thus acquired must be reserved for a history of the Gallery's Department of Modern Painting. It is evident from the additions made during the past hundred years that the ruling principle was no longer an aesthetic one, as it had been during the great eighteenth-century period of purchasing, but that choice of pictures was guided chiefly by historical considerations, in a deliberate attempt to fill the gaps in the collection.

Unfortunately, in those days, there were no really competent experts at Dresden with sufficient knowledge to enable them to make a proper assessment of the works offered for purchase. Thus, a number of Dutch paintings bought turned out to be only indifferent workshop products. Dresden could certainly have done with more pictures by Frans Hals; he is represented only by two tiny portraits, works bought in 1874 (Gal. nos. 1362, 1406) having subsequently to be eliminated as being merely by pupils. The same thing happened with Cuyp and Hobbema. And the twenty-three early Italian paintings from the collection of the Dresden painter Müller-Steinla, which came into the Gallery in 1857, proved to have usurped the resounding names they bore. Only a few, such as the fragment by the Master of the Bambino Vispo (Gal. no. 30), were found worthy of admission to the collection as representatives of late medieval work. In this respect the appointment of painters as directors of the Gallery led to unsatisfactory results.

Johann Friedrich Matthäi, who died in 1845, was succeeded as Gallery director in 1846 by Julius Schnorr von Carolsfeld, who had taught at the Munich Academy of Art; the transfer of the collection to Semper's building took place during his period of office. Schnorr's retirement came in 1871 and the post went to Julius Hübner, who had already served the collection as a member of the Gallery Commission. In 1856 he had brought out a catalogue in which the arrangement in the new building was described; despite a number of technical errors, it gives a clear idea of grouping and presentation. The most valuable feature of this catalogue is the introduction, which

69

relates the history of the collection for the first time, drawing on local source material.

The discussion as to the genuineness of *Burgomaster Meyer's Madonna*, by Holbein, bought at Venice by Algarotti–a copy to which Hübner wanted to give a privileged position equal to that of the *Sistine Madonna*–shows that the museum organization was in dire need of genuine experts.

The first of its directors to fulfil that need was Karl Woermann (1847–1933). Beginning his career in the law, he had gained recognition as an honorary lecturer on art at Heidelberg University in 1871, had been Professor of the History of Art and Literature at the Düsseldorf Academy since 1874, and had travelled extensively, building up by study and comparison the body of knowledge which was the best preparation for practical museum work. He took up his post at Dresden in 1882, after the death of Julius Hübner. In an autobiography written in 1924, he says that his administration of the Gallery 'immediately confronted me with a number of practical aesthetic problems ... to which I vigorously devoted myself.' The most urgent of these problems seemed to him to be the preparation of a detailed catalogue; this he regarded as the 'principal achievement' of his life. The first edition appeared in 1887. The biographies of artists it contained, and the attributions it made, were detailed and based both on Woermann's own knowledge and the most recent research. A brief but comprehensive description of each picture was also given, with particulars of its acquisition and quotations from the principal written evidence of its authenticity. In short, it provided for the first time what is nowadays expected of a scholarly catalogue.

Woermann classified the pictures according to their schools, as was then customary. He also numbered them consecutively, in an order that has been retained ever since. His outline of the Gallery's history goes much further than Hübner's so that his study is the necessary starting-point of all subsequent research. He also planned a complete rearrangement of the collection itself, declaring that he thought it advisable 'For reasons of scholarship as well as of art, to leave pictures of the same school and the same century side by side.' In the

70

last resort, however, he always put 'decorative requirements' before scientific ones, 'for a picture gallery is not a herbarium.'

In obedience to the *genius loci*, Woermann at first kept to Schnorr's and Hübner's method of hanging the pictures in rows, covering the whole wall. Gradually, however, it came to be accepted that a less crowded arrangement would do no harm to the general impression. Woermann began to consider the changes involved, 'but our efforts were defeated by opposition from the Gallery Commission. My esteemed successor was the first to be able to carry out the measures for which I had struggled and paved the way.'

This successor was Hans Posse (1879–1942). As soon as he took up his post, in 1910, he set about the rearrangement for which Woermann had been unable to secure permission. His aim was to show each picture to best advantage. In this he was guided by aesthetic considerations, though the historical principles of arrangement upheld by Woermann were retained and strengthened in his plans.

The rearrangement took several years. When the first World War broke out, the six large rooms on the first floor were ready. Next in turn came the small rooms along the north side of the Gallery. The walls, instead of being papered, were covered with woven material chosen to suit the pictures, which were now hung much further apart, Posse still kept them in two superimposed rows, but his arrangement was so sensitive that there was no impression of overcrowding. The original character of the collection was thus fully preserved.

Now that the pictures were wider apart, the problem of space again became acute. Posse decided to save room by removing all the modern paintings to a different building, and to spread the collection over into the two Zwinger pavilions abutting on the Gallery. One of these now housed the earliest German works, while the other received the French seventeenth- and eighteenth-century paintings. Pöppelmann's gay architecture made an ideal setting for Watteau and Lancret and for the collection of pastels.

The foundations for an extension of the Gallery were laid in 1916, but the work came to an end in the economic crisis of the post-war years, and the best had to be made of what already existed.

All this while Woermann went on with the scholarly side of his work in the Gallery. The last general catalogue was published in twelve editions in 1930, the artists' names being arranged in alphabetical order for the first time. Meanwhile Posse was preparing a detailed, scholarly catalogue in which every picture was to be reproduced and the accompanying notes were to make a point of describing the colours as precisely as possible. Here again, the paintings were classified according to schools. The first volume, which dealt with the Italian, Spanish and French pictures in the collection, was published in 1929. Preparations for the second volume, to be devoted to the Dutch and German pictures, were brought to an end by the second World War.

By this time, special attention was being given to the care of the pictures. Woermann had already put some of them, chiefly the smaller ones, under glass. Posse continued with this protective measure, though reflections, unavoidable in many cases, were annoying for visitors. Experienced restorers, supported by an Advisory Committee representing the Gallery, set to work on the paintings; one of them, Theodor Krause, dealt with the *Sistine Madonna* in 1931. In a report written 'to guard against the myths so often woven round famous works of art' and published in *Pantheon* (Vol. 8, p. 286), Posse declares that 'As the latest thorough investigation has confirmed, the *Sistine Madonna* is as wonderfully preserved as any four hundred-year-old painting on canvas could possibly be' – a state of things which has continued until the present day.

THE WAR, AND AFTER

On the outbreak of the second World War in 1939, the Gallery was closed. The removal of its contents took only a week. At first the pictures were stored on the ground floor of Semper's building, in the former Residence, and in two castles out in the country. Not until 1942 were they distributed among forty-five storage places at various distances from Dresden, where they were kept permanently under careful supervision. As during the Seven Years War, part of the collection went to the Castle of Königstein. Early in 1945, when the Russian armies were rapidly advancing, came an official order for the pictures stored to the east of the Elbe to be removed to depots lying further west. As a result they were exposed to the gravest danger, for their removal took place in winter, in bad weather, and sometimes under fire.

Thus it was that on the night of 13th February 1945 one of the lorries, with a load of 154 pictures, came to grief in the terrible air raid that reduced Dresden to rubble and ashes in the space of a few hours. The contents of this particular lorry were chiefly nineteenth-century paintings, including such celebrated works as Courbet's *Stone-breaker* (Gal. no. 2522). Among the older pictures that perished were Parmigianino's *Portrait of a Young Man as St Sebastian* (Gal. no. 162), Batoni's *Penitant Magdalena* (Gal. no. 454), two works by Magnasco (Gal. nos. 651, 652), the two large still-lifes by Weenix that Algarotti had bought in Venice (Gal. nos. 1666, 1667), and pictures by Cranach, Berchem, Pieter van Laer, Ryckaert, Savery, the elder Brueghel, Luca Giordano, Trevisani, Lanfranco, Barocci and many others. During the same raid, 42 paintings which, owing to their vast size, had been left in storage in the former Residence, were destroyed by fire; they included works by Guido Reni, Guercino, Solimena, Procaccini and Migliori.

Together with the Residence, the Frauenkirche and most of Dres-

73

den's other buildings of historical and artistic interest, this air raid destroyed Pöppelmann's Zwinger and Semper's adjacent Gallery. Strangely enough, one of the two paintings not removed for storage survived the hail of fire. This was the *Reception of a Lady of Rank*, by Montemezzano (Gal. no. 248 A), a fresco protected by sandbags in situ on the staircase. The other picture, by Louis Silvestre, too large for removal (Gal. no. 767), perished in the flames.

Despite the disastrous experience of this air raid, and regardless of all protests from the responsible museum officials, the order for the removal of the pictures from their various storage places was not countermanded. Apart from Königstein, the largest consignments were to go to the Albrechtsburg at Meißen and to Weesenstein Castle, near Pirna. In April 1945, immediately before the war came to an end, immensely valuable pictures were still being transported from their safely-guarded depots in the Albrechtsburg – declared, in an absurd last-minute announcement, to be a military fortress – to a railway tunnel near Pirna and an abandoned lime-pit near Pockau-Lengefeld. These pictures numbered about 250 in all, and included the *Sistine Madonna*, Titian's *Tribute Money*, and Dürer's 'Dresden' altarpiece.

Within a few days of the capitulation on 8th May, these pictures were rescued by special detachments of Soviet troops, and brought to safety. Even an hour's delay might damage the paintings irrepacably, owing to exposure to the weather and the breakdown of the electric heating for lack of current. First aid operations, particularly urgent in the case of the paintings on wood, were carried out on the spot. The pictures were then placed in the care of the Pushkin Museum in Moscow and the Museum of Eastern and Western Art at Kiev, where they remained for ten years. Among those needing special restoration were the *Tribute Money* and Francesco Francia's *Baptism of Christ*. One badly damaged picture – the central panel of Dürer's 'Dresden' altarpiece – was not dealt with in Moscow, the risks involved being so great that the decision as to what measures should be adopted was left to its German owners. The method finally chosen was based on the principle that Dürer's actual painting must not be tampered with

74

in any way whatsoever. All that was done where patches of the surface had been destroyed was to fill them in with neutral-toned watercolour and to efface a few of the worst scratches. The delicate task of re-backing the thin linen on which the picture was painted having been carried out to perfection, the colours appeared somewhat brighter and cleaner than before, and the drawing firmer, owing to the removal of traces of the paste used by Renner, who in 1840 had taken away the original clumsy wooden backing and replaced it with canvas, afterwards stretching the picture over a wooden frame.

When the pictures from the Dresden Gallery came back to Germany in the autumn of 1955, each of them was accompanied by a document giving precise details of the condition it had been in when first salvaged, the measures adopted for its security and restoration, and the state it was in when handed back to the committee of German experts which took over the pictures on their return. The first consignment reached Berlin on 12th October. The pictures which had been kept a Kiev were sent direct to Dresden.

The rebuilding of the picture gallery in the Zwinger had begun meanwhile. Clearance of the site was started on 8th June 1955, and the actual reconstruction on 29th June. Eleven months later the first section was complete, providing enough space for about two-thirds of the pictures. The Gallery was reopened on 3rd June 1956, the Dresden paintings having until then been on exhibition in the National Gallery in Berlin.

Work on the East wing and the central part of Semper's building was expedited by the fact that much of the masonry was still standing. The West wing presented a more difficult problem, for it had been entirely destroyed and had to be rebuilt from the ground up. This task was finished in the summer of 1960, so that the reconstructed Gallery could be opened to the public on 30th October of that year, four hundred years after the founding of the old *Kunstkammer*.

The new building faithfully reproduced Semper's façade, down to the smallest ornamental detail, and the internal structure also remained as before. A few unobtrusive but effective changes were made, however, to meet the requirements of modern museum technique. For

75

one thing, the four sides of the Rotunda were thrown open, transforming it from an ambiguous 'holy of holies' into a means of access to the second storey by way of an easy double staircase.

The line of rooms along the North side of the galleries became less like a succession of caverns because the partitions dividing them were now carried only half way up to the ceiling.

The cabinet of engravings having been removed elsewhere, the entire ground floor of the West wing became available for the Gallery. A large, artificially lighted room was built in the centre of it, to hold the Raphael tapestries. This wing is also used for lectures and concerts.

To protect the pictures from the danger of damp, the inside walls of the exhibition rooms were left unplastered in the new building, the hanging surface being faced with hardwood panels, and the upper part of the walls covered with plain material. The correct temperature is maintained by an up-to-date heating and ventilation system.

The new arrangement of the paintings follows the course of art-history much more closely than did the old system, though Woermann's warning that 'a picture gallery is not a herbarium' is not forgotten, and aesthetic considerations take precedence whenever a compromise becomes inevitable. The new arrangement also aims at displaying the special characteristics of the Dresden collection, reflecting the vicissitudes that marked its formation rather than trying to conceal them.

The final requirement was to bring the new features into harmony with Semper's architecture, and the following arrangement has now been adopted. The Italian paintings hang in the first-floor gallery to the west of the Rotunda, and the Dutch pictures in the corresponding gallery to the east. The room situated between the Rotunda and the Theaterplatz entrance contains the French works, thus forming a wedge between the schools of art to the north and south of the Alps.

The new system focuses attention on three outstanding masterpieces. Raphael's *Sistine Madonna* hangs on the end wall of the main gallery in the West wing, and the large picture from Vermeer's early period in the corresponding position in the East wing. The central hall in the middle section of the Gallery – at the point of intersection with the Rotunda – contains Nicolas Poussin's *Flora*.

76

The Dresden Gallery owes its fame to the wealth of late Renaissance and Italian and Dutch baroque paintings it possesses. These sections, in keeping with their importance have been placed, with the work of the seventeenth-century French masters, on the first floor.

The smaller groups are arranged in chronological order in the other parts of the Gallery. The second floor houses the eighteenth-century pictures—Italian and French in the East wing, German in the West wing. The Spanish pictures hang in the central portion, reached by stairs leading up from the Rotunda. As the small but choice quattrocento group had hitherto been slightly cramped, it was thought better to give it more space in two small ground-floor rooms where the quiet beauty of the pictures can be seen to the best advantage.

The other small group, the early German and Dutch paintings, remains where it was in Posse's time, in the Zwinger pavilion at the east end of the Gallery, the ground floor of which now houses the restorers' workshop.

The South gallery, which faces the top of the main staircase, provided an ideal setting for Bernardo Bellotto's views of Dresden. These harmonize very well with the architecture of the Zwinger building, which visitors can see from the large bay windows.

The corresponding South gallery in the West wing is used for temporary exhibitions of works taken from the reserves. It also contains showcases in which the restorers' workshop displays material illustrating its activities.

The modern principle of hanging the pictures in a single row has been observed throughout, with very few exceptions. One such exception is in the Rotunda, which contains several large Italian and Flemish works for which it would have been difficult to find space elsewhere; they include a hunting picture by Snyders, Rubens' *Quos Ego*, Matthäus' *Madonna*, Carracci's *Assumption of the Virgin*, and pictures by Guido Reni, Trevisani and Chiari. The seventeenth-century Dutch and Flemish 'little masters' are also, in some cases, hung in two superimposed rows, to make their abundance more evident. So far as possible all the works of a particular artist are hung together. This rule is only broken where the difference in size is too great—

77

as in the case of Annibale Carracci's *St Roch*, which had to be hung in a separate room at the far end of the West wing.

The work of the lesser Dutch masters of the seventeenth century are grouped according to subject, an arrangement facilitated by the specialization so characteristic of that period. Thus, the individual cabinets display landscape paintings, portraits, still-lifes, architectural views, and bourgeois or peasant genre painting. Only the two great masters, Rembrandt and Rubens, with the most important of their pupils, are grouped together in three main rooms of the East wing. The new arrangement allows for the exhibition of 610 pictures in all. This is barely a third of the total number transferred from the 'Stables' in the middle of the last century. The remaining works are stored in the reserves.

Paintings of the nineteenth and twentieth centuries, including contemporary works, are exhibited in Pillnitz Castle in the eastern outskirts of Dresden, in a gallery opened soon after the end of the second World War to show such pictures as had remained at Dresden.

A catalogue with brief notes on the works by old masters exhibited in Semper's building is available for visitors. The scientific cataloguing of the entire collection is still in progress.

It seems almost more important to bring out a complete list of pictures lost during the second World War; for apart from those destroyed in the air raid a number of others vanished, chiefly those which had been lent to decorate public buildings in Dresden and elsewhere. This task is complicated by the fact that most of the loan agreements were burnt. The complete list will ultimately be published as a catalogue, illustrated with reproductions.

The foregoing outline of the Gallery's history, which traces it back to the early days of the *Kunstkammer*, could never have been written without the help of the extensive research carried out by art experts and historians. In the interests of readability the author thinks it better not to list the individual sources on which he has drawn. He wishes, however, to offer his thanks to all those concerned, and more especially to those who preceded him as directors of the Gallery.

78

THE PLATES

FRANCESCO COSSA (*c.* 1435 –1477)
ANNUNCIATION   Panel
Gallery No. 43   Height 137 cm. (53⁷/₈")
                                                             Width 113 cm. (44¹/₂")

Under a richly carved portico, through which we look out into the street
beyond, the Angel of the Annunciation kneels in front of Mary. She has
come out of her room to hear the strange message, and stands listening,
with meekly bent head. At her feet a snail from the vineyards, the emblem
of virginity, crawls across the stone-paved floor.

The time-honoured Bible story had inspired countless artists since the
early Christian period. In the fifteenth century it was treated realistic detail.
Northern painters often set the scene indoors, in a cosy room, while in
the southern countries, where most of the day is spent out of doors, it was
more often placed in the street in front of the Virgin's house.

Francesco Cossa looks at the world with the eager, fascinated eyes of the
boy portrayed by Pinturicchio, and is thus a typical painter of the Early
Renaissance. He shows us every detail of the splendid architecture, the
coloured marble with its lavish carving, the houses in the background. The
day of realistic street scenery has not yet come, and the buildings here seem
to have been assembled from unrelated pieces, like a stage set. But there are
signs of keen observation. The effect is sometimes capricious, almost comic,
as when the angel's halo, instead of floating free, is securely fastened to his
head by a metal support. The law of cause and effect was beginning to
prevail over the spirituality of medieval times.

But that is of no importance compared with the artistic quality of the
picture. Naive it may be, but its strength and its bewitching ingenuity are
as undeniable as its firm structure, in which the figures stand like statues
against their background. The picture was bought – as a Mantegna – from the
Chiesa dell' Osservanza at Bologna, by Canon Luigi Crespi in 1750.

80

ANTONELLO DA MESSINA (*c.* 1430–1479)
THE MARTYRDOM OF ST SEBASTIAN   Transferred from wood to canvas
Gallery No. 52   Height 171 cm. (67$^3/_8$")
                                                        Width 85.5 cm. (33$^5/_8$")

Antonello's Sebastian stands with his hands tied loosely to a tree; above him
is a bright blue sky, where big white clouds are drifting. Five arrows project
from his well-proportioned body, but his face expresses melancholy rather
than physical pain. The Italian painter shows no trace of the pious ferocity
displayed by contemporary German artists. His graceful nude is more like
a Greek god than a Christian martyr, and the suggestion of classical times
is strengthened by the broken pillar that lies at the Saint's feet. This is an
art based on observation of nature combined with the study of the antique.

The figure stands in a space surrounded by bright and simple architectural
constructions. Antonello takes an obvious delight in applying the rules of
perspective, which had been discovered not long before this time. He has
deliberately chosen a very low vanishing-point, to which the lines of his
picture slope down clearly and steeply. The sleeping figure on the ground is
boldly foreshortened and shown almost frontally, like Mantegna's *Dead
Christ* in the Brera at Milan.

Two couples, seated high up on a balcony hung with carpets, gaze
placidly down at the square where the cruel performance has just taken
place. A few other people stroll on their way or stand in conversation,
showing little or no interest in what is happening.

The pillar-like chimneys on the crenellated roofs are characteristic of
Venice, where the artist spent the last few years of his life. The wonderfully harmonized colour-scheme also suggests Venice, while the luminosity
of the individual colours reminds us that when at Naples Antonello probably came into contact with the art of Jan van Eyck. By his treatment of
the misty blue distances in the background, which already exploits atmospheric effects, Antonella shows affinities with Piero della Francesca.

82

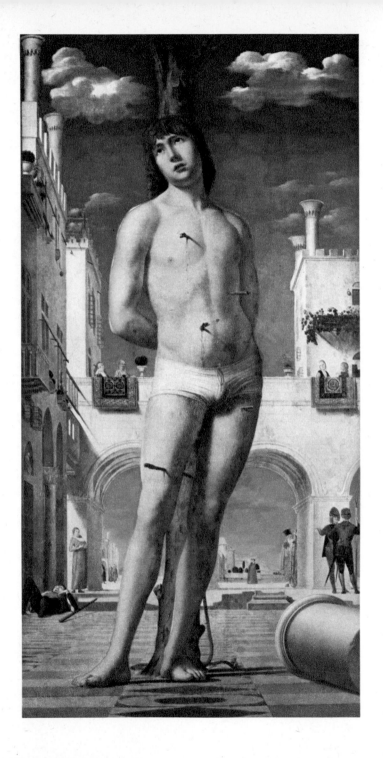

ANDREA MANTEGNA (1431–1506)

THE HOLY FAMILY   Canvas

Gallery No. 51   Height 75.5 cm. (29⅝")
                                                        Width 61.5 cm. (24⅛")

The Virgin is gently supporting the little body of the Child, as he stands
in her lap with one arm round her neck. Their eyes do not meet, and yet,
with their heads so close together they convey a sense of spiritual closeness
which is something new in quattrocento art. To the left of the group is
Joseph and to the right, Elizabeth, whose little son, John the Baptist, stands
in front of her, leaning against Mary's knee. He is pointing at the Christ-
child, and holds up a leafy cross in allusion to the Saviour's death. Round
his arm is a band with the inscription, (EC)CE AGNUS DEI – Behold the
Lamb of God.

The picture has a kind of austere charm, not due solely to the restrained
gestures of the figures and their grave, intense faces. Its composition is an
equally important factor.

The personages are shown in clear-cut relief against a neutral ground,
and grouped in such a way that they seem all to be on the same plane.
This creates an impression which is usually confined to figures in the round –
not surprising when we realize that Mantegna's work was strongly influenced by Donatello, the greatest of fifteenth-century sculptors, and so learnt
much from the art of ancient times. Thence he derived the principle of
Isokephalia, according which to the heads in a composition must all be at
the same level. Joseph's head has a particularly classical aspect, in its resemblance to the portrait bust of some Roman Emperor.

The picture is a network of intersecting lines – horizontal, vertical and
diagonal – which give it a firm structure reflected in the harmonious grouping.
The colour is handled in accordance with this inner logic, producing a
deep, calm glowing effect from which the brighter portions stand out gently,
mitigating the almost excessive precision of the drawing.

This work was bought from the heirs of Charles Eastlake, in London,
in 1873.

84

FRANCESCO FRANCIA (*c.* 1450–1517)

THE BAPTISM OF CHRIST   Panel

Gallery No. 48   Height 209 cm. (82″)

Width 169 cm. (66″)

Francesco Francia's *Baptism of Christ* seems to mark the point at which the quattrocento artists turned their searching gaze from the contemplation of detail and suddenly began to view the scene before them as a whole, from a greater distance. The components of the picture are still sharply outlined, so that each individual object is seen as distinct from the others, seldom or never overlapping its neighbour, and the figures are all placed on one level, for clearer visibility. The illusion of depth is produced not intuitively, but deliberately, thanks to a few curves which recede into the distance.

The colour, too, still obeys fifteenth-century principles; it is harsh, clear and brilliant, more like a coloured drawing than a painting. The Jordan water resembles a pane of cold blue glass, in which the figure of Christ is reflected as he stands in it. Medieval practice is recalled by the use of gold in the haloes and in the landscape.

Yet for all this, the novel features of Francia's picture are evident. Despite its preoccupation with detail, there is something monumental about it. The meticulous imitation of nature in which earlier artists had delighted has been reduced for the sake of the general composition, which builds up to a magnificent pyramid.

The same monumental effect was achieved in that century by several other outstanding painters, such as Masaccio and Piero della Francesca. But in their case there is an archaic, remote quality. Francia is more human, more lyrical. The inclination to personal expression had slowly developed in the quattrocento; here we see it as an accepted feature of artistic creation. Francia stands on the threshold of a new period, the Late Renaissance.

On the picture is written in gold letters: FRANCIA. AURIFEX. BON. F. M. V. VIII (Francia the goldsmith painted this picture in 1509).

86

SANDRO BOTTICELLI (1445–1510)

FOUR SCENES FROM THE LIFE OF ST ZENOBIUS

Gallery No. 9

Panel

Height 66 cm. (26″)

Width 182 cm. (71⅝″)

In this picture Botticelli relates consecutively, like a medieval artist, the story of a boy who was run over by a cart, killed, committed to the care of a holy man with a reputation for miracle-working, brought back to life and restored to his fortunate mother.

The miracle-worker was Zenobius, Bishop and patron Saint of Florence. He died in the year 417. On the right he is shown again, on his deathbed, surrounded by a pious group which kneels to receive his last blessing.

This picture is one of a series dealing with the life of St Zenobius, two of the others being in the National Gallery and one in the Metropolitan Museum, New York. Their oblong shape suggests that they were painted to decorated a chest *(cassone)*, though as they are not of uniform size they

88

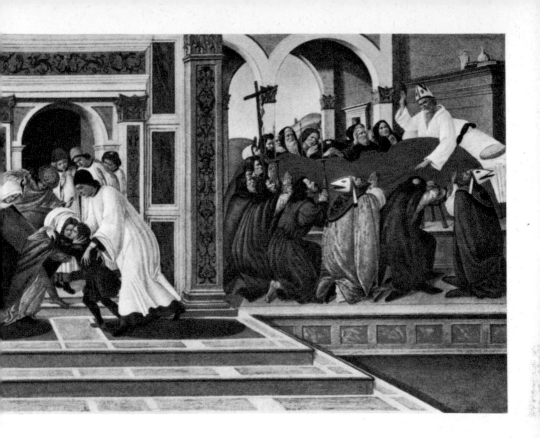

may have been used as wall panels. Botticelli painted his Zenobius series after 1500, at a time when he was passing through a spiritual crisis brought on by the terrible execution of Savonarola (1498). The Grecian charm of his youthful years and his mature period had given way to a tense and gloomy mood which resulted in an even more conservative style, when it did not preclude creative work altogether.

Other *cassone* painters of the period also produced narrative pictures. But the bright, translucent colours, the firm architectural structure, the clear-cut differentiation of the groups of figures and the meagre landscape in the background are all typical of the early quattrocento. The picture has a strange, taut vitality which is the reverse of naive. Everyone seems to be in desperate haste. Even the praying figures have an air of dropping to their knees in the nick of time. There is a wild abandonment of grief on some of the faces.

This picture was acquired from the Quandt collection, Dresden, in 1868.

89

BERNARDINO PINTURICCHIO (1454–1513)
PORTRAIT OF A BOY   Panel
Gallery No. 41   Height 50 cm. (19⁵/₈")

Height 50 cm. (19$^5/_8$")
Width 35.5 cm. (13$^3/_4$")

The boy is looking straight out of the picture – gazing solemnly, rather dreamily, into the novel and alluring world that lies before him. He does not yet feel, as would an adult, a direct, natural relationship with what he sees. His immature face wears a reserved, slightly defiant expression; even the eyes seem to look inward. The hands, often so revealing, are not visible. The plain red doublet is fastened up to the throat. Only the boy's hair belies to some extent his prim features; it falls, thick and silky, from beneath his blue cap, down to his shoulders. Behind him a landscape stretches into blue distances, with graceful trees, smooth water and a town. The chaste prettiness of the scene is in keeping with the childishness of the figure in the foreground.

This work is typical of the Early Renaissance artist and the enchanting new world he was beginning to explore, at first tentatively, then with optimistic enthusiasm. Everything is regarded objectively, everything has significance, the colour is smooth and pure.

Such a receptive attitude can only stem from a special reverence for man as individual, and this results in an independent style of portrait painting. The demands made on the painter are manifold, for he seeks not only to portray the sitter's outward appearance, but to read and reveal character. In this picture Pinturicchio has achieved these aims and he also gives a convincing representation of a particular time of life, that of the boy approaching young manhood.

The painting is first mentioned in the inventory for 1722, where it is ascribed to an 'Imitator of Raphael'.

90

GIOVANNI BATTISTA CIMA (1459/60–1517/18)

PRESENTATION OF THE VIRGIN

Gallery No. 63

Panel

Height 105 cm. (41³/₈")

Width 145 cm. (57¹/₈")

Cima was born at Conegliano, a little town in the province of Treviso. Like Titian, he came from the foothills of the Alps, and like him, he worked in Venice. Both painters modelled themselves on Giovanni Bellini, the greatest of the Venetian Early Renaissance artists, though Cima was never to exceed the limitations of the quattrocento.

During this period Venice had far-reaching trade relations, particularly with the East. Many picturesque, curiously-clad figures from distant lands passed before the keen eye of the painter. The turbaned orientals Cima met with in his daily walks lent this picture a realistic local colour he must have welcomed; for the men of his day, with their delight in the senses and in the world around them, liked to see even the holy events of the Bible in everyday dress. Truth to nature was still only episodic, however; the broad view and the complete synthesis were not achieved until the next generation. Cima's oriental figures suggest Jerusalem, but the mountains in the background of the picture are those of the Alps he had seen throughout his childhood.

An indescribable charm emanates from the little still-life—a bird in a cage, eggs and bread in a basket, which a boy has spread out on the steps that lead up to the temple. The sharp angles of the steps give the artist full scope to display his gift for structural clarity.

This powerful theme, which dominates the picture, was used later by Titian—to far grander effect—in his large painting on the same subject, now in the Accademia at Venice. He also uses the Alpine landscape.

According to tradition, this picture comes from a church near Venice, where it was bought in 1743. In the inventory for 1754 it is ascribed to Bellini.

92

LORENZO DI CREDI (1459/60–1537)

MADONNA AND CHILD WITH TWO SAINTS   Panel

Gallery No. 15   Height 117.5 cm. $(46^{1}/_{2}'')$

Width 176   cm. $(69^{1}/_{4}'')$

Lorenzo di Credi was a Florentine and a pupil of Andrea del Verrocchio, who had taught his craft to the young Leonardo da Vinci. Verrocchio himself had been apprenticed to a goldsmith, and was sculptor as well as painter.

This versatility is characteristic of artistic practice in the quattrocento. The trained sculptor's hand may be discerned behind the figures in many paintings, so strongly modelled from light and shadow, and the goldsmith's skill is revealed in much of the intricate decoration.

These influences are evident in the panel by Lorenzo di Credi reproduced here. His figures might be rubbings from brass. The arched buildings amid which they are so convincingly set are decorated with sharply-drawn ornamental work. In the foreground, as though within hand's reach, is a magnificent metal vase containing a bunch of flowers, each of them easily identifiable. This kind of still-life, more common in early German and Flemish art, bears witness to the strong feeling for nature which was prevalent everywhere at the time.

This is unmistakably a sixteenth-century picture. The unsophisticated charm of painters such as Francesco Cossa has been left far behind, and the monumental character of Late Renaissance painting lies far ahead. The figures in this work of Credi's old age are delicate and a little stilted. The colours are translucent, limpid, with pale pink, greens and blues dominating.

The picture came from the Barker collection in London and was bought for Dresden in 1874.

94

PALMA VECCHIO (1480–1528)
THE MEETING OF JACOB AND RACHEL   Canvas
Gallery No. 192   Height 146 cm. (57")
                                                          Width 250 cm. (98")

The Bible tells us that Jacob was forced into exile as the result of a quarrel
with his elder brother about the latter's birthright. The fugitive came to
the district where his uncle Laban, a wealthy owner of flocks, possessed
extensive grazing-grounds. Beside a well to which the cattle were brought
to water he met Laban's daughter, Rachel, for whose hand he was to spend
fourteen years as herdsman in his uncle's service. On telling each other
their names, the cousins realized with delight that they were related.

This is the moment chosen by Palma Vecchio for his picture. Jacob and
Rachel have drawn close, to take hands, and Rachel is offering her cousin
her cheek to kiss. A sheepdog is barking excitedly at the stranger, whose
staff and knapsack lie at his feet. Behind them are the animals and a trough
into which a herdsman is pouring water from a wooden bucket. A second
herdsman is seated on the rim of the well, gazing at the cousins with a
devoted expression.

There is a bucolic atmosphere about the scene. The broad valley, with
its shady trees, lies in the calm of evening. Winding paths lead to the
wooded heights above. The hilltops are crowned with fortified villages.
A range of mountains shuts off the dim, blue distance. Birds are flying in
the cloudy sky. Warm golden light pervades the place.

Palma has given landscape a new importance. The Early Renaissance
painters introduced realism by abandoning the gold background of medieval
art, introducing the spectator to open, three-dimensional space. But they
had shown their figures against a scene, not within it. Palma is the first
to show people amid their surroundings. True, he does not paint landscape for its own sake; for him it is still only scenery. But his pleasure
in the representation of nature is evident, he is fascinated by the novelty
of his subject.

The picture came to Dresden from the Casa Malipiero in Venice, and
is mentioned in the Guarienti catalogue (before 1753) as a 'Giorgione', with
the number 438.

96

RAPHAEL (1483–1520)

The Madonna di San Sisto, or 'Sistine Madonna'   Canvas
Gallery No. 93   Height 265 cm. (104^1/$_8$")
                                                 Width 196 cm. (77^1/$_8$")

The curtain falls back. Haloed in radiance, the Madonna steps down over a carpet of clouds, with the naked Child on her arm. As she moves, her cloak billows up from her shoulder and the hem of her robe swings sharply to one side. Mother and child are gazing into the distance. Pope Sixtus II, who was burnt as a martyr in the reign of the Emperor Valerian, kneels in gorgeous vestments beside the Virgin, gazing up at her and pointing downwards, towards the spectator, with his right hand. Opposite him kneels St Barbara, turning a little aside. Her attribute, the tower in which she starved to death for her faith, is just visible. Two cherubs are leaning, with childish simplicity, over the parapet in the foreground.

Raphael's famous picture is a wonderful, airy harmony of movement and repose, majesty and humility, devotion and withdrawal, gravity and dreamy playfulness. Even the colours contribute to this play of contrasts, with their balanced complements – red and green, blue and yellow – and their finely differentiated scale of cold and warm tones. All the lines are simple curves. A sense of repose is created by the pyramid-shaped composition formed by the separate figures. This picture is the purest expression of the Late Renaissance ideal, brought to perfection by Raphael.

Vasari tells us that the work was painted for the high altar of the church at the monastery of San Sisto, Piacenza, whose patron saints were the two who are shown kneeling before the Madonna. And from there, through the agency of Abate Giovanni Battista Bianconi, it was purchased for the Dresden Gallery in 1754, for the sum of 2,000 ducats, by Augustus III, who had seen and admired the picture in its original location when he visited Italy as a youth.

ANDREA DEL SARTO (1486–1530)
THE SACRIFICE OF ABRAHAM   Panel
Gallery No. 77   Height 213 cm. (83⅞")
                                                            Width 159 cm. (67⅝")

Isaac is seen bent forward, with one knee resting on the sacrificial stone,
while his father Abraham holds his hands behind his back. The knife that
is to serve for the sacrifice God has required as a token of obedience is
already drawn. But the Angel is swooping down from heaven to cut short
the preposterous operation, and the scapegoat is already at hand.

Many artists have taken up this theme at different times. Rembrandt goes
furthest in depicting the mysterious combination of blind devotion, pain,
love, self-mastery and trust finally rewarded. Subjective psychology of that
kind is not within the reach of Andrea del Sarto. As a typical Late
Renaissance painter, he centres the drama on objective law, and Abraham,
achieving greatness through superhuman obedience, is the dominant figure
in the picture.

The technical methods inherited from the previous generation, especially
anatomy and perspective, have been unobtrusively developed, and now seem
to be used without effort. Sarto's use of bold, simple contours has avoided
the confusion which might have resulted from the oblique composition
– adopted for the sense of space it conveys – the sweeping gestures and the
intersecting lines.

The colours are muted to a warm harmony employing few tones.

The influence of classical antiquity still pervades the design. Isaac's
naked figure might have come from the Laocoon group, which was already
celebrated. Several preliminary sketches by Sarto are preserved in the
collections of drawings at Florence and Stockholm. The artist has signed his
painting with his monogram, 'AA'. According to Vasari, it was painted about
1530 for Francis I; it passed into the Duke of Modena's collection in 1649,
and thence to Dresden in 1746.

100

CORREGGIO (1494–1534)

HOLY NIGHT (detail)   Panel

Gallery No. 152   Height 256.5 cm. (100³/₄")

Width 188 cm. (74")

It is night. On the far horizon, the faint glow of dawn of can be seen beyond a range of mountains. The newborn child lies on straw in a ruined building of classical aspect, sheltered by a wooden roof; his mother leans over him. Light radiates from the group, illuminating the shepherds who are arriving from one side and a cloud of angels above their heads. It is so dazzling that the youngest shepherd, who carries the basket with the gift of doves, is shading his eyes with his hand. Joseph stands in the background, attending to the ass. Beyond him are other figures, half-perceived in the dark landscape.

There is something festive about the light, in keeping with the chorus of angels; it suggests an exultant burst of song, or a motet by Mozart.

Correggio's life was short and oppressed by poverty und care, in utter contrast to the sweetness and charm of his art. Always, even when dealing with religious subjects, he seems to be doing homage to the sensual magic of existence. He pours out a stream of new, stimulating ideas, which were not paralleled until far into the seventeenth century. The problem of light, which is treated in an entirely new way in this picture, was to be the foremost concern of such artists as Caravaggio and Rembrandt, while assymmetry and the use of diagonal lines in pictorial composition, like the complicated grouping of figures with bold overlapping and foreshortening, or the portrayal of bodies hovering in the air, were problems the Baroque painters set themselves to solve.

Correggio painted this picture for the Pratoneri Chapel in the church of San Prospero, at Reggio. The fee was to be 200 Lire and the contract was signed in October 1522, but the work was not done until 1530. In May 1640 the picture passed into the Duke of Modena's collection, and thence, in 1746, to Dresden.

102

PARMIGIANINO (1503–1540)
MADONNA OF THE ROSE
Gallery No. 161

Panel
Height 109 cm. (43″)
Width 88.5 cm. (34³/₄″)

The Virgin is stretching out one hand to take a rose the Child is offering her; the other hand is laid, as though protectively, on her lap. The very independent Child is leaning his head, with its elegant curls, not on his mother's shoulder but on a nearby table which is overed with a cloth. His hand, with its coral bracelet, rests on a shiny, bluish-coloured globe.

Raphael's simple dignity, sublimity and tender humanity are evidenced in the clear, uncomplicated structure of his picture; Parmigianino turns the ancient theme of Virgin and Child into something complicated. The composition seems over-ingenious. The folds of the thin robes fall into spiral curves, and the unnaturally slender hands have long, pointed fingers. The Virgin's head is bent, but the curiously unchildlike infant is gazing rather apathetically at the spectator, who is tempted to forget that this is a religious work. This lends probability to Vasari's story that when Parmigianino began to paint the picture for Pietro Aretino, the insolent poet, at Bologna, he first intended it to be a Venus and Cupid. The theme was altered later, when it was decided that the painting was to be given to Pope Clement VII.

The painting and draughtsmanship are extremely meticulous, the colour cool and subdued.

Parmigianino died young – at the age of thirty-seven – after a roving life, in Parma, the town of his birth. The influence of Correggio, Raphael and Michelangelo is merely incidental to his very independent course of development. His studio was the meeting-place of the fashionable, quick-witted youth of his day, the period of mannerism that intervened between Late Renaissance and early Baroque.

The *Madonna of the Rose* was bought for Dresden in 1752 by Luigi Crespi from the Casa Zani at Bologna. Two preliminary sketches for it are now in the collection of engravings at Budapest.

GIROLAMO DA CARPI (1501–1556)
OPPORTUNITY AND PATIENCE   Canvas
Gallery No. 142   Height 211 cm. (83$^{1}/_{8}$")
                                                    Width 110 cm. (43$^{1}/_{4}$")

Storm-clouds darken the sky. In the grey light a wavy-haired stripling is travelling on a ball along the edge of a chasm. In his uplifted right hand he holds a knife. The veiled figure of a woman half turns towards him.

The theme is an ancient one, which can be traced back to classical times. The youth is Occasio – Opportunity – always hurrying by and difficult to seize. The knife has several meanings. Sometimes it symbolizes the right weapon for those who are bold enough to try to grasp Occasio. At other times it is the emblem of indecision, of those whose resolve always hangs by a thread when determination is called for. The woman symbolizes Patience, whose help is indispensable to those prepared to wait until Occasio appears.

This picture was painted during a period addicted to antiquarian fantasy, pedantry and obscure, complicated allegories, whose imagery was often familiar to only a few people. The figure of Occasio, for instance, is reminiscent of Fortune and her wheel, which may account for the strangely androgynous aspect Carpi has given to it.

Fortune, however, comes in a happily-awaited, auspicious hour, whereas there is something uncanny, almost demoniac, about this Occasio. The note of danger is echoed by the abyss into which the rash may so easily fall. The black clouds, too, look somehow threatening. This pessimism is typical of many sixteenth-century manneristic works.

The picture was painted for the Ducal Court of Ferrara in 1541. Later it passed to the Modena collection and thence, in 1746, to Dresden. There is a preliminary sketch in the Budapest Museum.

106

GIORGIONE (1477–1510)

SLEEPING VENUS

Gallery No. 185

Canvas

Height 108.5 cm. (42½")

Width 175 cm. (68⅞")

In the quietly falling dusk, Venus is asleep. She lies in a flowery meadow, her head resting gently on one upraised arm. There is something musical in the flow of lines that plays around her body, and the colour scheme is attuned to it. The composition is dominated by a deep harmony of red and green, against which her ivory-white skin seems to glimmer. The landscape, stretching away into softly-outlined distances, is redolent of peace. Everything seems to have withdrawn into itself. One feels that this picture never expected to be looked at.

When Giorgione died in Venice at the age of thirty-three, during an epidemic of the plague, he left in his studio a number of unfinished pictures, including a sleeping Venus which, says tradition, was completed by Titian, who added a Cupid and the background landscape.

It is true that there was once a little Cupid at the feet of the Dresden Venus; he was painted out later, being regarded as too obtrusive. And the landscape is identical with the one used by Titian in his *Noli me tangere,* now in the National Gallery in London. But it cannot be definitely proved that the Dresden picture is the one mentioned by tradition. There are divergent views as to the respective shares of the two artists in the famous painting. Many scholars go so far as to deny that Giorgione began it.

There was, indeed, a close relationship between these two painters. In 1508 they were working together on the frescoes in the Fondaco dei Tedeschi at Venice. Giorgione, who must have had a fascinating and mysteriously charming personality, brought a contemplative and very individual element into the art of his period. All his pictures have an indefinably musical quality (quite absent from Titian's work). Their iconography is often obscure. The fourteenth-century harshness still to be found in Bellini was left far behind by Giorgione, who may thus be regarded as the initiator of Late Renaissance painting in Venice.

The *Sleeping Venus* was bought for Augustus the Strong, from the French dealer Le Roy, in 1699. In the 1707 inventory it appears as 'Giorgione, original', while in that of 1722 it is attributed to Titian.

108

TITIAN (*c.* 1477–1576)
THE TRIBUTE MONEY   Panel
Gallery No. 169   Height 75 cm. (29^1/$_2$")
                                             Width 56 cm. (22")

The tempter approaches and enquires whether or no it is right to pay taxes to the Emperor. By way of reply, Jesus asks to see a coin, indicates the Emperor's portrait upon it, and utters the famous words 'Render unto Caesar the things which are Caesar's, and unto God the things which are God's.' This maxim was engraved on the gold coins issued by the Duke of Ferrara, for whom Titian painted the *Cristo della Moneta.*

For all its calm objectivity, the picture draws life from the tension of mysterious contrasts which give a dramatic element to the scene. Christ is seen almost full face, his features radiating tranquillity and confidence, in juxtaposition with the sharp profile of his questioner, and the rough, closed hand that holds the coin is close to Jesus' open one with the pointing, authoritative finger. The Pharisee has a dark brown skin, while his opponent's complexion is clear and his features are refined. The contrast is heightened by the colours of their clothing.

Vasari complained that Titian's 'draughtsmanship' was deficient, and there is some justification for the charge. The Florentine critic forgot, however, that a picture may be developed from pure colour, without the aid of line. And there lies the outstanding virtue of Titian, that masterly colourist. His natural tendency may have been accentuated by the immaterial atmosphere of Venice, which heightened the value of colour.

Titian's career follows a definite pattern, and can be divided into sharply-defined periods. Changes of colour-scheme help to distinguish one period from another. *The Tribute Money* was painted at the end of Titian's early period, which is marked by the same love of contrasts that characterizes the *Cristo della Moneta.*

The picture is signed TICIANUS. F., on the right side of the Pharisee's collar. According to Vasari, it was painted for a cupboard door in the palace of Duke Alfonso of Ferrara. Early in the seventeenth century it found its way to Modena, whence it was taken to Dresden with the rest of the Duke's collection.

110

TITIAN (*c.* 1477–1576)

PORTRAIT OF A LADY IN WHITE

Gallery No. 170

Canvas

Height 102 cm. (40$^{1}/_{2}$″)
Width 86 cm. (33$^{7}/_{8}$″)

It was believed at one time that the sitter was Titian's daughter Lavinia and that the little flag she holds was an indication of her recent marriage. But a fan of this kind was no more than an article of fashion, which women, irrespective of age and social position, were wont to use in any circumstances. Moreover, there is another portrait of Titian's daughter, and the two are so unlike that they obviously do not represent the same person. Perhaps the suggestion of intimacy the artist has put into this picture led to the mistake, for despite the modesty of her manner, the young woman's eyes look out at the spectator with an expression of confident understanding.

There is an air of luxury about the anonymous beauty, with the shimmering silk of her dress and her wonderful pearls. White and gold predominate in the colour-scheme. The soft pink of her complexion gives her face a vivacity which is enhanced by the dark background against which it is set.

Titian was one of the greatest portraitists of all time; and while his rendering of surface textures in itself arouses our enthusiasm, his hand could add depth to the human face as well, even when, as in this instance, he was simply paying homage to physical beauty.

In earlier times this picture was repeatedly copied. Van Dyck's Chatsworth sketchbook contains a drawing made from it. Rubens tried his hand at it too, as we see from a copy by him which is now at Vienna. The original came to Dresden from the Duke of Modena's collection, in 1746.

112

JACOPO TINTORETTO (1518–1594)

The Archangel Michael fighting Satan · Canvas

Gallery No. 266

Height 318 cm. (125^1/$_4$″)
Width 220 cm. (86^5/$_8$″)

The clouds draw apart, and God the Father, radiant in glory, appears in the highest heavens. Bright rays of light pierce downwards to strike the Evil One, as he strives to raise his many heads. St Michael with his host of angels is already attacking, thrusting the enemy into the abyss with his mighty lance. Tranquilly above the clouds hovers the Madonna, with the Child in her arms and her foot resting lightly on the virginal crescent of the silver moon.

Tintoretto's composition is based on Chapter 13 of the Book of Revelations, where Satan in described as a seven-headed monster and St Michael as the champion who defeats all evil powers.

The whirlpool of movement formed by all these falling and writhing bodies has an oppressive effect, a suggestion of chaos. But the artist succeeds in imparting clarity to the dramatic scene. The shaft of the angel's spear forms a powerful axis along which the separate figures are rythmically disposed.

Light plays a great part in Tintoretto's work, especially in his later period; here it lends a spiritual aspect to the battle scene, which takes on a mysterious translucency.

Even the colours in this picture are pervaded by light, which transfigures all substances represented there. Transparent, muted shades of yellow and green predominate, their chilly glow warming to a marvellous hyacinth-mauve.

Tintoretto is fond of depicting vigorous hovering figures; the theme is used already in the first of his major works, which brought him fame – the *Miracle of St Mark*, painted in 1548, now in the Accademia in Venice.

However ethereal, however far-fetched he may appear at times, this artist never loses touch with reality. He attached great importance to drawing and composition. We know that he made studies of Michelangelo's statues. He also used to make small, accurate models for the crowd scenes in his large paintings.

This picture is first mentioned in the Dresden inventory of 1754. How it came to Dresden we do not know.

114

JACOPO TINTORETTO (1518–1594)

PORTRAIT OF TWO MEN   Canvas
Gallery No. 270   Height 99.5 cm. (39$^1/8$")
                                             Width 121 cm. (47$^5/8$")

This picture is listed in an early inventory with the title '*Meister und Discipel*' (*Master and Pupil*). For lack of fuller particulars, this literary-sounding name was later abandoned in favour of the non-commital *Portrait of Two Men*.

The original title has a ring of truth about it, all the same. It conveys a sense of the spiritual bond momentarily uniting the old man and the youth. We feel a question has been asked, and now awaits an answer. And here the roles of the odd pair are reversed; it is not a case of the teacher laying down the law while the pupil listens submissively. This time the younger man has taken the initiative. He seems to have put forward some quite original, unexpected idea, and his mentor has to think for a moment before replying to it. The elder man is listening, tense but alert, frowning slightly, his left hand gripping the arm of the chair. The pupil is completely absorbed in his idea.

The scholar's black gown has something monkish about it, but it is not too austere. There is a suggestion of the Socratic dialogue about the scene, which reminds us that a Platonic Academy had been founded in Florence a century before, under the patronage of Cosimo de' Medici.

A sense of impermanence and excitement are characteristic of Tintoretto, even when dealing with spiritual subjects. The regal Titian, his great contemporary and rival, would never have left a picture in this state of unresolved tension. He, a faithful observer of the spiritual and social hierarchy, used contrasts only to create a feeling of repose and balance, never to point a conflict.

Tintoretto's picture came to Dresden in 1749 from the imperial collection at Prague.

116

PAOLO VERONESE (1528–1588)
THE MARRIAGE AT CANA   Canvas
Gallery No. 226   Height 207 cm. (81$^1/_2$")
                                                         Width 457 cm. (179$^7/_8$")

The marriage feast is taking place on an open terrace with a background of
sumptuous architecture. The guests sit at table, while servants hurry to and
fro carrying spits and silver dishes laden with rich food. Children cluster
round the seats, one charming group consisting of a lad playing with his cat.
Wine is being poured from heavy earthenware pitchers. The steward of the
wine cellar, in a shimmering silk cloak, stands erect, tasting red wine from
a shallow glass. He is the first to catch the eye. And amid all the showy
throng one almost fails to realize that the figure halfway along the table
is Jesus. There is a halo round his head, at the sight of which we are reminded
that this is no ordinary feast, but the marriage at Cana, when the water was
turned into wine.

It is by no accident that the spectator is not immediately brought to the
point. The Renaissance artists were coming more and more to use the
traditional Christian themes as a pretext for depicting scenes from everyday
life. And is this not a feast in a rich man's house? In this case Veronese's
secularization of his subject is evidenced chiefly by the fact that Jesus, whom
an earlier painter would have placed alone in the centre of the composition,
is here shown as one of a group and set to one side of the picture. He is still
the central figure of his own group, but the emphasis has unmistakably
shifted.

This development is largely explained by the fact that an increasing
number of wealthy patrons – and not only the Church, as formerly – were
now commissioning pictures, and they wanted to see themselves and their
world in the paintings created for them.

This is one of a series of four large pictures painted by Veronese for the
Cuccina family, which remained until the seventeenth century in their
Venetian palace (now the Palazzo Papadopoli). The others represent the
Adoration of the Magi, Christ carrying the Cross, and the Cuccina family
themselves, praying to the Virgin.

In 1645 Duke Francesco I of Modena acquired the four pictures for
his gallery, and from there they came to Dresden in 1746.

118

PAOLO VERONESE (1528-1588)
THE FINDING OF MOSES   Canvas
Gallery No. 229
Height 178 cm. (70¹/₈")
Width 277 cm. (109")

Veronese came two generations after Titian. The achievements of the great Venetian masters of the Late Renaissance find their place in his work as accepted features, effortlessly introduced.

Ideas from the circle of Parmigianino and Giulio Romano are adapted as well, without subduing Veronese's glowing colour or chilling his lively inventiveness. Intellectual asceticism and the fondness for the 'Concetto' characteristic of the mannerist painters were entirely alien to him.

Despite his lavish treatment of his subjects, every detail is given its own, unmistakable significance. His natural talent for the formal treatment of large masses was probably strengthened by his period of residence in Rome, and it is thus not surprising that his later works should begin to display the features that were to characterize Baroque painting in the following century.

Veronese was a painter who gave a festive atmosphere to everything he touched upon. Even so comparatively unostentatious a happening as the finding of Moses becomes a brilliant, courtly event under his brush. Pharaoh's daughter, surrounded by her companions, gazes at the baby which has just been rescued from the water and is now being shown to her by two girls, one kneeling, the other bending towards her. An impression of space, gaiety and liveliness is created by the surrounding dogs, dwarf, halberdiers, the woman in the right hand lower corner holding the basket in which the

120

baby was found, the royal coach waiting at the edge of a wood, and the city on the far side of the river.

There is plenty of scope here for Veronese's love of rich materials and fine jewels. The deep, glowing colours are softened by the silvery light. The individual figures are arranged with admirable mastery in groups that combine to produce the impressive effect of the whole work.

This picture came to Dresden in 1747 from the Casa Grimani de' Servi in Venice.

121

ANNIBALE CARRACCI (1560–1609)
PORTRAIT OF THE LUTE-PLAYER GIOVANNI GABRIELLE   Canvas
Gallery No. 308   Height 77 cm. (30¼")
                                                         Width 64 cm. (25¼")

The long history of portraiture is one of continual expansion. Not only were the sitters' unique, individual features scrutinized with increasing penetration and portrayed with growing skill; psychological traits, too, were brought to light and rendered with a more subtle touch. The subjects were depicted each in his own sphere – it became a matter of course for the scholar, the merchant or the military commander to appear in characteristic guise, as well as the princes and patrons for whom portrait-painting had so long been reserved.

Here Annibale Carracci has given us the picture of a musician. Gabrielle was a personal friend of his. Studies preserved in Vienna and Florence show that this was intended as an unmistakable portrait. The musical atmosphere had grown familiar during this period, for in Italy music had now taken its place side by side with the plastic arts. The madrigal, that song-form, came to full bloom about 1600, and the lute was the most popular instrument for chamber music until the second half of the seventeenth century, when it was ousted by the clavichord and the harpsichord.

Here the artist has given a minutely detailed and expert representation of that instrument, with its eleven strings, its pear-shaped body, the smooth, light-coloured wooden surface with the beautifully carved rosette as its sound hole and the wide, flat-set neck.

Yet this portrait of a musician is not exactly musical; it has something austere, something classical about it. All sound is stilled. It seems as though Gabrielle had ceased playing and was sitting motionless, firm as a statue, posing for his friend the painter.

This classicism is a conservative element in Carracci's work. It came as a salutary restraining influence upon artistic development in that period of bold experiment with form. But it represents only one side of the painter, who sometimes reveals himself as a surprisingly daring innovator – as, for instance, in his landscape and genre paintings.

The *Lute-player* came to Dresden in 1746, from the Duke of Modena's collection.

122

BERNARDO STROZZI (1581–1644)
GIRL WITH A VIOLA   Canvas
Gallery No. 658   Height 126 cm. (49⅝")
                                                             Width 99 cm. (39")

The girl is leaning on a table, a far-away look in her eyes, as though she
were listening to the final notes of the piece that has just ended. She is
still holding her instrument, a tenor viol, in one hand.

The picture is built up from deep, sonorous colour harmonies. Everything is subdued. Lingering vibrations are slowly dying away, and the
colour values, too, recede by degrees. The only touch of brightness comes
from the woman's brick-red dress. The flesh-tones are luminous, but more
restrained.

The player's features are so individual that she cannot have been intended
as an impersonal figure, an allegorical representation of Music. But we
do not know her name. There may possibly be a clue in the sheet music,
which has a real song inscribed on it.

Bernardo Strozzi was a native of Genoa, where Rubens is believed to
have spent some time in 1607. Even if one did not know this, the woman's
voluptuous form would bring the great Flemish painter to mind. But her
unconcerned attitude, with its touch of slightly theatrical showiness, its
suggestion of the prima donna, speaks of a southern land entirely alien
to Rubens. It lacks the ultimate infusion of spirituality which pervades
and distinguishes even Rubens's most daring scenes.

Algarotti bought the picture for Dresden from the Casa Sagredo in
Venice in 1743.

124

DOMENICHINO (1582–1641)
St Sebastian
Gallery No. 319

Canvas
Height 138.5 cm. (54^1/$_2$″)
Width 94 cm. (37″)

Sebastian was an officer of the Imperial bodyguard in the reign of Diocletian. He was sentenced to death for helping persecuted Christians, and executed in the Flavian Amphitheatre in Rome. But though pierced by many arrows, he was not killed. A woman convert to the new faith took care of him and nursed him back to life. As soon as he was recovered, he lodged an indictment against the Emperor, reproaching him for his hostility to the Christians. Thereupon he was again arrested, and executed. His tomb is beside the Via Appia.

The arrow is the traditional symbol of sudden misfortune, particularly in the form of illness. Sebastian had a miraculous escape from death by this weapon. So it seemed natural to choose him as protector against the plague, which in those days of rudimentary medical knowledge was endemic and periodically carried off thousands of victims.

Sebastian was a favourite subject for artists from the earliest Christian times. He is usually depicted, naked except for a loincloth, tied to a tree and pierced with arrows, as we saw in the picture by Antonello da Messina.

The sculptural calm imparted to his figure of the Saint by that early Renaissance painter has now – a hundred and fifty years later – given way to the impassioned gesticulation seen in Domenichino's picture. The youthful martyr's body leans backwards, his arms and legs flung out. But his expression is one of gentleness rather than torment. Here again, all movement is moderated by a latent classicism. The quiet, sombre colouring of the landscape in which Domenichino has set the martyrdom is in keeping with its indefinable lyricism.

The picture was bought for Dresden from Le Leu, in Paris, about 1750.

126

DOMENICO FETTI (1589–1624)
The Return of the Prodigal Son   Panel
Gallery No. 417   Height 60 cm. (23⁵/₈″)
                                                     Width 45 cm. (17³/₄″)

A tendency towards the monumental was evident in Italian art from the very first, and genre painting never developed to the extent that characterized the Netherlands in the seventeenth century. A powerful and restrictive influence over the choice of subjects was exercised, moreover, by the Catholic Church, which in Fetti's day was still an important source of commissions. So it is not unnatural that even when a painter wanted to depict a scene of daily life, he should turn to the Bible for suggestions.

The parable of the Prodigal Son was a favourite choice in such circumstances, and was used as a pretext for secular pictures even in medieval times. A series of from four to seven paintings would show the son leaving home, squandering his money in foreign lands and then earning a meagre living as a swineherd, until at last he finds the courage to return home and ask his father's forgiveness. The seventeenth century usually confined itself to depicting the last scene, the homecoming. The supreme example is Rembrandt's, in which the full depth of the parable is revealed.

Fetti's little painting is comparatively artless and obvious. He sets the scene in a palatial arcaded building similar to that in which Veronese had placed his *Marriage at Cana*. The son is kneeling on the steps in front of his father, whose arms are round him in a forgiving embrace. Several people are approaching from either side, to join in the occasion. There is nothing particularly moving or edifying in the event, so we are left free to admire the fresh, natural atmosphere engendered by this unconstrained little masterpiece. The composition is vaporous, the colours bright and fluid; the brushwork intimates rather than defines, but the intention is unmistakable throughout. Thus it is that Fetti enriches the art of his time with touches of impressionism.

The picture came to Dresden from the imperial gallery at Prague in 1742, with seven other illustrations of parables painted by Fetti in this same genre style.

128

GUERCINO (1591–1666)

ST FRANCIS IN ECSTASY   Canvas
Gallery No. 356   Height 162.5 cm. $(63^7/8'')$
                                            Width 127 cm. $(50'')$

St Francis has come to a lonely spot so that he can read the Scriptures undisturbed. He is in a ruined building of classical times, and is seated on a fallen pillar. The place is a barren waste, with only one almost leafless tree growing amid the scattered ruins. Suddenly a dazzling light shines down and the sound of a violin is heard. The Saint has turned away in alarm and shielded his face with his hands. So he does not see the violin-playing angel who is floating down on a white cloud. It is the heavenly music and not the vision that has amazed and confused him. His wasted features bear an expression of rapture. Guercino has succeeded in imparting tense excitement even to the landscape. The horizon is bathed in cold light which shines on a distant fortress. The sky overhead is darkening with the approach of night.

The range of colours is small – earthy brown, olive green, dark blue and the bright light, which maintain the ascetic atmosphere of the theme itself. Yet every stroke of the brush is winged with a fervour that imparts itself even to the smallest details of the picture. The lines flow softly, smoothly, as though in response to the irresistible harmony of the violin.

Heat and cold, remorseless severity and gentle devotion, intellect and emotion, intermingle here without attaining complete harmony.

The picture was bought for the Dresden Gallery from the Casa Ranuzzi at Bologna in 1756.

CARLO DOLCI (1616–1686)
THE DAUGHTER OF HERODIAS   Canvas
Gallery No. 508   Height 95.5 cm. ($37^{1}/_{2}''$)
                                                            Width 80.5 cm. ($31^{5}/_{8}''$)

Salome is elegantly dressed in a silk gown, with a necklace of pearls nearly
as big as cherries. She is holding high, in both hands, the chased silver
dish in which the head of John the Baptist has been placed, but her face is
turned aside and her expression is melancholy. Looking at her beautiful but
rather insipid features, one can hardly believe that it was she who laid the
cunning plot to which John fell victim.

Carlo Dolci was much admired in his own day as a painter of agreeable
pieces for collectors. The popularity of this particular work, which may
have sent an agreeable shudder down the spine of the beholder, is attested
by the fact that replicas are to be found in the Uffizi, at Glasgow, in
Windsor Castle and elsewhere.

The artistic conventions of the late nineteenth century found Dolci's
work equally acceptable. Many of the churches built during that period
selected for their altarpiece a copy of his Last Supper, the original of which
is likewise in the Dresden Gallery.

Nowadays his fame seems to be under a cloud, and his work is either
stored away in the reserves of galleries or used to illustrate a particular
phase in the history of art collecting.

Yet it is only fair to pay tribute to the exceptional, effortless mastery
of his composition. Equally remarkable here is the treatment of colour,
where he has confined himself almost entirely to subdued tones of olive
green and blue.

The picture was acquired for Dresden through de Brais, from the
Carignan collection in Paris, in 1742.

132

CARLO CIGNANI (1628-1719)
JOSEPH AND POTIPHAR'S WIFE

Gallery No. 387

Canvas

Height 99 cm. (39")
Width 99 cm. (39")

Potiphar's wife is trying to draw the youthful Joseph into her embrace. Joseph, obedient to God's command, is extricating himself from her tempting arms, but has lost his cloak during the brief struggle. She will use this as evidence to have Joseph thrown into prison.

The moral of the biblical story could hardly be clearer. Cignani turns it into an erotic scene of fortuitous charm. One is not entirely convinced by the pious expression on the youth's face, and the gesture with which his hands are warding off approach looks stylized rather than serious. Besides, the charms of the lovely young woman are so lavishly displayed that they detract from the spectator's interest in the outcome of the story.

The sensual element in Italian religious art became increasingly evident after the beginning of the sixteenth century. With Cignani, the sense of intimacy has definitely gained the upper hand and the religious character of the original theme is forgotten.

The introduction of the profane atmosphere has been accompanied by a departure from the earlier simplicity of composition. The restful, remote atmosphere which still characterized religious painting in the Late Renaissance, giving it dignity and conviction, has slowly evaporated.

Cignani's work displays very subtle mastery. Though the oblique lines of his composition are imposed upon the figures, the effect is not forced, but appears perfectly natural and in keeping. The outline of the group is broken up in a number of ways; for instance Joseph not only raises his arms, he spreads his fingers out as well.

The colour is rich, magnificent and luminous. Diagonal composition, dynamism and sensuality are characteristic of Baroque painting, and all three are combined in Cignani's picture. Underlying them, however, is a classical feeling, recognisable in the precision of draughtsmanship and modelling applied to the whole. The influence of the school of Carracci can be seen here.

Cignani painted the picture for Contarini, Procurator of St Mark's, Venice. It was bought by Guarienti for the Dresden Gallery in 1749.

134

GIUSEPPE MARIA CRESPI (1665–1747)

THE SACRAMENT OF CONFIRMATION   Canvas
Gallery No. 395   Height 125.5 cm. (49³/₈")
                                                    Width 93 cm. (36³/₈")

The white-robed bishop, leaning on his crosier, is bending towards the child who kneels before him with hands clasped in prayer, and anointing his forehead. The godfather kneels beside the boy, his right hand outstretched to touch him lightly on the shoulder. An acolyte stands on one side, holding the dish.

The subject is handled with the simplicity of a genre painting, and yet an inner force radiates from it. On closer examination each individual figure seems so powerful that it threatens to burst from its narrow setting.

The representation is confined to essentials, to the simple acts of religious observance wherein all the participants are united by selfless piety.

The scene is not defined, there is no architectural setting; but it conveys, for all its remoteness from the world, a feeling of fortuitousness and spontaneity. Two of the figures are partly cut off by the edge of the picture, and the priest in the background turns aside and gazes absently into space. Two worlds are thus brought into relationship – the sacred or dedicated and the profane or incidental.

The colour is heavy, almost monochrome. Crespi has wrought everything out of an earthy, brownish tone. The lights have the bright sheen of molten lead. One contemporary critic reproved the artist for this peculiarity. To a present-day spectator it seems more like an indication of future developments, of something that reappeared in the art of the late nineteenth century.

This painting is one of a series depicting the Seven Sacraments. Crespi painted them in 1712 for Cardinal Ottoboni, of Rome, and it was in that city that Augustus III bought the whole set for the Dresden Gallery, in the middle of the eighteenth century.

136

GIOVANNI BATTISTA PIAZZETTA (1682–1754)

THE YOUNG COLOUR-BEARER   Canvas
Gallery No. 571   Height 87 cm. (34^1/$_4$")
                                            Width 71.5 cm. (28^1/$_8$")

The boy is leaning nonchalantly against a stone balustrade, holding the
shaft of a banner in his right hand. His head, seen in profile, is slightly
bent. He is gazing absently into space.

The theme is a simple one, halfway between portrait and genre painting.
Yet for all its naturalness, the picture possesses a certain grandeur. Perhaps
the youth is the winner of some contest. Even in its late period, Italian
painting retained its sense of the monumental, evidenced as early as Pinturicchio's *Portrait of a Boy*, where the firm, concentrated outline has a
statuesque quality.

Piazzetta was a pupil of Crespi. Clearly he has a predilection for scenes
of everyday life. Occasionally he produces an effect of pertness or slight
frivolousness, such as the rococo period favoured. But his sprightliness is
always subdued by his colour-scheme, which is grave and sonorous. He
is fond of harmonies of dark blue, green and reddish-brown, brightened
by shimmering white. This combination is used in the present picture. The
range of shades is indescribably rich. The boy's profile, rising out of deep
shadows, is effectively set off by the white flag behind it. This is yet another
of the wonderful feats resulting from the Venetian sense of colour.

Count Algarotti bought the picture for the Dresden Gallery in Venice
in 1743. It was thus purchased as an example of contemporary painting – a
fact which may not immediately occur to the present-day spectator.

138

ANTONIO DA CANAL, known as *CANALETTO* (1697–1768)
VENICE, SS. GIOVANNI E PAOLO   Canvas
Gallery No. 582   Height 125 cm. (49¹/₄")
                                                   Width 165 cm. (65")

The church of SS. Giovanni e Paolo, and the square on which it stands,
are bathed in bright sunshine. The sharp outlines of the architecture seem
to be softened by a faint mist. The huge brick structure of the basilica
casts a deep shadow over the façade of the Scuola di San Marco. On the
right Verrocchio's Colleoni sits his horse. Weeds grow in the cracks between
the stones. Washing hangs to dry outside the windows. A few people are
standing about in groups, others are bustling to and fro. In the background
the Rio dei Mendicanti, spanned by the graceful curve of a bridge, leads
away towards the Fondamente Nuove, where Titian's house stood, with
the wide, smooth expanse of the lagoon at the far end. Islands lie there,
scarcely rising above the surface of the water that mirrors them – San
Michele with its tower, keeping watch over the burial ground; Murano,
Burano, Torcello; and on a clear day, perhaps, the snow-capped chain of
the Alps can be seen in the far distance.

This is far more, of course, than we can see in Canaletto's picture. But
we sense the background, whence the wind blows across the city, with a
tang of salt in its breath – a wind charged with the atmosphere which has
inspired generations of artists to fresh efforts, ever since Canaletto taught
them, in his inimitable way, to perceive the boundless magic of Venice.

True, Canaletto is concerned primarily with topographical features. But
if we compare his pictures with the skilful, matter-of-fact and often rather
arid *vedute* painted by his nephew, Bernardo Bellotto, we see that the
distance between Canaletto and the ethereal impressionism of – for instance – Francesco Guardi is not, after all, so tremendous.

This is a work from Canaletto's early period. It makes its first appearance, with two other Venetian views by him, in the inventory for 1754.

140

BERNARDO BELLOTTO (1720–1780)
VIEW OF DRESDEN FROM THE RIGHT BANK OF THE ELBE   Canvas
Gallery No. 606   Height 133 cm. ($52^3/8''$)
                                         Width 237 cm. ($93^1/4''$)

Bernardo Bellotto, a pupil of his uncle Antonio da Canal, came to Dresden from Venice and worked there as Court painter from 1747 to 1766. He was commissioned by Augustus III to paint a series of *vedute* of the city, and they combine the artist's imaginative approach with a high degree of realism. This was the period when the Gallery was acquiring its finest works, and Dresden itself was the scene of the building activities from which it emerged looking much as it does today.

As part of this process the cramping medieval fortifications were pulled down, in order to give a clear view along the river front. Magnificent buildings were erected, grouped in such a way as to produce a new and exceptionally interesting skyline.

Bellotto conveys this admirably in a general view painted in 1748. The peculiarity of his interpretation is that it gives a Venetian air to the scene. The broad surface of the Elbe reminds us of the Grand Canal. Daniel Pöppelmann's bridge, with its bold curve, suggests the Rialto, and the great dome of the Frauenkirche recalls such buildings as Santa Maria della Salute. None of this can have been unintentional.

The tower of the Catholic Hofkirche, designed by Gaetano Chiaveri, is still surrounded by scaffolding, for the church was not yet quite finished. So that in addition to its artistic value, this picture is of considerable interest where the history of architecture is concerned.

Bellotto's paintings lack the atmosphere that is such a characteristic feature of the city views painted by his uncle, Canaletto. The drawing and colour are hard and the record so meticulously detailed as to smack of pedantry. They foreshadow the approaching period of bourgeois classicism.

This picture came into the Dresden Gallery in 1754.

142

ALBRECHT DÜRER (1471–1528)

CENTRE PANEL OF THE DRESDEN ALTARPIECE: Canvas
THE ADORATION OF THE INFANT JESUS   Height 107 cm. (42$^{1}/_{8}$")
Gallery No. 1869   Width 96.5 cm. (37$^{7}/_{8}$")

Elector Frederick the Wise of Saxony, for whom Lucas Cranach worked at Wittenberg, had sat to Albrecht Dürer at Nuremberg in 1496 for a portrait which is now in Berlin. It was probably on this occasion that Frederick commissioned the painting known as the *Dresden Altarpiece,* which was brought to the Dresden *Kunstkammer* in 1687 from the castle church at Wittenberg.

The technique adopted by Dürer was the same in both cases; he painted in watercolour on thin linen.

In this picture Mary bends reverently before the Child as he lies on a parapet between two pillars. To one side stands a lectern with an open book lying on it. The narrow room with the view from its window, and the door opening into Joseph's workshop seems as it were to have been forced into the surrounding framework. The artist does not yet quite know how to combine his figures with their background.

He makes a point of drawing upon the impressions of the visit to Italy from which he has just returned, making use of perspective and showing his forms in the round. But these calculations do not spoil the general impression of quiet sincerity. The intimate mood is deepened by the treatment of details, which is suggestive of a still-life painting.

This is further enhanced by the little angels which swarm all over the picture. One tiny creature is fanning the flies away from the sleeping Child's face with a whisk. Others are sweeping and cleaning the room. Two are holding a beautifully wrought crown above Mary's head, while another pair are energetically swinging censers.

Many late-medieval characteristics survive in this work, though an attempt to absorb the great innovations of form is evident in its over-all treatment. The difference of size between the holy figures and the host of serving angels, for instance, is reminiscent of the medieval method of indicating relative importance.

Dürer's colours are delicate, with the flatness of fresco painting. His work has survived unchanged in the side panels, but the central picture was considerably painted over at a later period.

144

ALBRECHT DÜRER
(1471–1528)   Canvas
WINGS OF THE DRESDEN
ALTARPIECE: ST ANTHONY
AND ST SEBASTIAN
Gallery No. 1869   Each:
Height 114 cm. (44$^7/_8$″)
Width 45 cm. (17$^3/_4$″)

The parapet that runs across the central painting of the retable is extended to the side panels in such a way as to serve as a pedestal for the figures of St Anthony and St Sebastian.

Both these saints were regarded as protectors against the plague and other scourges.

Dürer had fled to Italy from Nuremberg in 1495 to escape the plague, and this may account for his taking St Anthony and St Sebastian as the secondary figures in the first important picture he painted after his return.

The bearded, stern-featured hermit stands with his hand on a large book, while the youthful Sebastian turns in prayer towards the Virgin and Child in the central panel. His muscular torso display the arrow wounds that brought him martyrdom. When Dürer painted this picture he was only about twenty-five years old and can have had no very great experience of life. So it is all the more remarkable that he should have sensed and rendered so convincingly the antithesis between

146

youth and age, and used it to give spiritual rhythm to his composition. The contrast between the eager, extrovert enthusiasm of the youth and the withdrawn wisdom of the old man is a spiritual reflection of the external differences between their naked and clothed bodies.

Even in this early work, Dürer thus reveals his continual search for a synthesis between depth of human feeling and majesty of outward form.

The little angels scattered over the centre of the altarpiece appear on the side panels as well. Some are doing battle with horrible-looking monsters, while others carry crowns destined for the heads of martyrs and others who have withstood persecution for their faith.

The painting came to the Dresden Gallery in 1867 from the Schlosskirche at Wittenberg.

147

ALBRECHT DÜRER (1471–1528)

PORTRAIT OF A YOUNG MAN   Panel

Gallery No. 1871   Height 45.5 cm. (17$^1/_8$")

Width 31.5 cm. (12$^3/_8$")

Dürer brought back a great number of portraits from his visit to the Netherlands, made in 1520/21, when he was fifty years old and at the height of his powers. They commemorate the stimulus of personal intercourse with interesting and widely-travelled men.

Now that he was in full command of his technique, Dürer had no difficulty in evolving a matured, self-contained style of his own out of the already highly developed Dutch art of portraiture. Indeed, the method he had already used in his earlier years (a bust on a pedestal) had long been familiar to early Netherlandish artists.

The surprising element in Dürer's painting is its vitality. The young man in this portrait seems as though he wished to break out of the frame, and is restrained only by centripetal forces. The eyes that gaze at us above the prominent cheekbones are catlike, but not unfriendly. The left hand holds a sheet of paper, the right, with sharply foreshortened fingers, rests on the parapet at the lower edge of the picture thus strengthening the impression of nearness.

The plain, reddish-brown background combines with the dark tone of the fur-trimmed gown to emphasise the calm expression of the face.

It has been suggested, on the strength of an entry made by Dürer in the journal he kept on his Dutch travels, that the sitter may have been the painter Barent van Orley, but it is more probably a certain Bernhard von Resten.

Dürer has signed the picture with his monogram and dated it 1521. It was probably acquired for Dresden through Le Leu in Paris.

LUCAS CRANACH THE ELDER (1472–1553)
DUKE HENRY THE PIOUS AND HIS WIFE,
CATHERINE OF MECKLENBURG
Gallery No. 1906 G H

Transferred from panel to canvas
Each:
Height 184 cm. (72$^{1}/_{2}$″)
Width 82.5 cm. (32$^{3}/_{8}$″)

Duke Henry the Pious (1473–1541) was one of the Saxon rulers who helped to spread Martin Luther's reform in their own lands. His wife (1477–1561) also joined the new movement, though at first secretly. They appointed one of Luther's sympathisers as Court preacher at an early stage of the Reformation.

Lucas Cranach, too, was a Protestant. For many years he served the royal pair as Court painter, and produced many portraits of them and their children.

These two, dating from 1514, are life-size. The portrait of the Duchess is dated, and bears the artist's initials and the mark of his workshop, a winged serpent.

The figures are painted very flat against a black background which gives full decorative effect to the colours and the rich gold employed.

The Duke is crowned with a wreath of pinks in two colours, while his consort wears a splendid plumed hat. Each of them has a dog; at the Duchess's feet sits an elegant watchdog with a knowing expression, while a borzoi gambols round the Duke.

Both portraits have a sophisticated charm that belies their apparent naivety. The magnificent costumes look like metal, and surround the bodies of their wearers as though with protective armour. The first impression is purely ornamental. Only gradually do we realize that the stiff, mask-like features have a pensive, almost weary expression.

These portraits were in the original *Kunstkammer*. They appear in the inventory for 1641. In 1905 they were transferred to the Picture Gallery from the History Museum.

151

LUCAS CRANACH THE ELDER (1472–1553)
Sᴛ Cᴀᴛʜᴇʀɪɴᴇ Aʟᴛᴀʀᴘɪᴇᴄᴇ
Gallery No. 1906

Centre panel: Height 126 cm. (48⅝″), Width 139.5 cm. (54¾″)
Side panels: Height 124 cm. (46″), Width 66.5 cm. (26″)

Catharine of Alexandria was a learned young lady who succeeded in refuting, and converting to Christianity, fifty philosphers sent by Maxentius II to argue against her. The infuriated Emperor thereupon threw her into prison and left her to starve; but his aim was defeated by angels who brought her food. After that he ordered her to be broken on the wheel; but

152

fire from heaven destroyed the instrument of martyrdom. So as a last resort, the steadfast maiden was beheaded. St Catherine became the patron saint of learning, and her legend was thus of special interest to the Renaissance, with its great intellectual vitality. By 1505, at the latest, Lucas Cranach was working as Court painter of Frederick the Wise at Wittenberg, where a university had been founded in 1502. The St Catharine altarpiece, which is dated 1506, undoubtedly has some connection with that event.

The right wing of the altarpiece shows Saints Dorothea, Agnes and Kunigunda; the left wing Saints Barbara, Ursula and Margaret, with the fortress of Coburg in the background. First mentioned in the 1835 catalogue.

153

HANS BALDUNG, CALLED GRIEN (1484/5–1545)
MUCIUS SCAEVOLA   Panel
Gallery No. 1888 B   Height 98 cm. (38⅝″)
                                               Width 68.5 cm. (26⅞″)

During Rome's disastrous war against the Etruscan King Porsena, a daring
Roman, Mucius Scaevola, made an unsuccessful attempt to assassinate the
enemy leader. Scaevola was captured, and attempts were made to bribe him
into treacherous disclosures. But in vain. To demonstrate his steadfastness,
he thrust his right hand into a fire of coals and held it there to be burnt,
thus gaining eternal fame as a symbol of Roman virtue.

Hans Baldung, known to his friends as Grien, sets the scene in a military
camp of his own day. King Porsena, protected by a group of Etruscan
guards – bearded troopers, with halberds and lances – is conducting the
interrogation. Mucius Scaevola's blow did not fall on the King, but on
another Etruscan leader, who supports himself against a stone bench

The steadfast Roman stands erect beside the brazier, in the act of
thrusting his right hand into the flames. He has been allowed to keep his
weapon – a sword. He gazes with fierce determination at the King, whose
attitude is curiously detached.

In the background we see the walls and towers of a very German-looking
Rome. Clouds lower in the sky.

The colour scheme is very luminous – red, green and an almost garish
yellow. Despite its naive composition, the picture expresses resolution and
passionate feeling.

This is one of a series of five paintings illustrating ancient legend and
history. Baldung took his themes from books such as the *Gesta Romanorum*,
and from Italian engravings. German Renaissance painters often derived
their material at second hand in this way; but they handled it with great
independence and originality, infusing into their pictures considerable
classical erudition.

The work is signed and dated: H. G. BALDUNG FAC 1531. It was
bought from a private owner in Paris for the Hackenbroch collection, and
came from there to the Dresden Gallery in 1927.

154

HANS HOLBEIN THE YOUNGER (1497–1543)

DOUBLE PORTRAIT OF SIR THOMAS GODSALVE AND HIS SON JOHN   Panel

Gallery No. 1809   Height 35 cm. (13³/₄″)

Width 36 cm. (14¹/₈″)

The double portrait involves special problems for the painter, which explains why it did not make its appearance in the history of portraiture until the painting of individual portraits had been thoroughly mastered. By 1528, when Holbein painted Sir Thomas (1481–1542, notary, of Norwich) with his son John (1510–1556), he himself was a mature artist and this style of portraiture already had a long tradition behind it.

The problem is, how to fit two different sitters into one pictorial composition, while preserving their individual physical characteristics. In Holbein's portrait the sitters are an elderly man and a youth, father and son, and despite their relation by blood, very different in appearance and personality. The family likeness is seen in the powerful nose, so much the most prominent feature of both faces that, especially in the case of the son, it even seems to dwarf the forehand. The father's features are vigorous but restrained, with compressed lips and sharp eyes; the son's face is altogether vaguer, gentler and less firmly characterized.

The differences between the two models are brought out by the way they are placed, both looking in the same direction. Here again the son seems to be following the lead of his father, who displays his authority not only in his manner, but physically, by partly hiding the boy with one shoulder. Their clothes have a unifying effect; both are plainly dressed, with fur-lined cloaks showing a glimpse of white linen underneath.

All this builds up a harmonious effect, but one in which a wealth of the most delicate overtones provides the differentiation required to stimulate the spectator's mind.

The picture was acquired for the Dresden Gallery in 1749, through Le Leu in Paris.

156

HANS HOLBEIN THE YOUNGER (1497–1543)
PORTRAIT OF THE SIEUR DE MORETTE   Panel
Gallery No. 1890   Height 92.5 cm. (36³/₈")
                                                Width 75 cm. (29¹/₂")

German painting developed in the fifteenth and sixteenth centuries with so
many ramifications and on so many different levels, that it is hardly possible
to include it under the heading 'Renaissance art' in the straightforward sense
in which that term can be applied to Italy. It often seems as though
German art developed without transition from its late medieval phase into
certain forms of Baroque. Indeed, this exceedingly fruitful and original phase
has been more aptly named 'the art of Dürer's time', after its most eminent
exponent.

But there was one artist who so perfectly embodied the spirit of the
Renaissance that his work is sufficient in itself to represent the values
contributed by German art to that great stylistic period in Europe.

It was by no mere accident that in the Duke of Modena's collection,
from which it came to Dresden, Holbein's portrait of Morette was attributed
to Leonardo da Vinci. Not so much because the treatment shows a slight
– though entirely superficial – resemblance to the alleged self-portrait by
that great Italian genius, but because the impression conveyed is one of
humanity raised to a rare level of fulfillment. Holbein seems to have looked
beyond the ephemeral characteristics of his model and created a being of
universal validity. The preliminary drawing, preserved in the Cabinet of
Engravings an Dresden, is far more spontaneous, individual, personal. In the
painting the whole effect is firm, convincing, timeless, monumental. The
self-assurance of the great man, so typical of the Renaissance, radiates from
this portrait.

The painting has richness. The materials – silk, fur, supple leather and
magnificently chased metal – are rendered in all their splendour. Holbein's
purely technical skill is astounding, quite apart from his intellectual grasp.

The sitter, Charles de Solier, Sieur de Morette, was French envoy to the
English Court in 1534, which helps to date the picture. It came to Dresden
from the Modena collection in 1746.

158

ADAM ELSHEIMER (1578–1610)
LANDSCAPE WITH THE FLIGHT INTO EGYPT   Copper
Gallery No. 1978   Height 17.5 cm. (6⁷/₈″)
                                                    Width 22 cm. (8⁵/₈″)

Adam Elsheimer died at the age of thirty-two in Rome, far from his German home, unrecognized and destitute; he left little work behind him, but that little was to exercise a quiet yet concentrated influence upon the development of art. Not only did Rubens acknowledge a debt to him, but his treatment of light influenced Rembrandt and details of his figure composition were taken up by later Dutch painters such as Jordaens, Brouwer and Adriaen van Ostade.

Elsheimer's greatest merit however, lay in the impetus he gave to the development of landscape painting as an independent branch of art, which came into its own about 1600 in Rome among artists such as Annibale Carracci, Domenichino and Paul Bril.

It was the early Renaissance painters who began to introduce landscape as a background to their religious pictures – the way having previously been paved by drawing and engraving. Nevertheless it was a long time before landscape came to be regarded as a worthy theme for an entire picture. Even with Elsheimer the incidental figures were still so important that they determined the title of the work – as in this Dresden example, *Landscape with the Flight into Egypt.*

Palma, too, sets his meeting of Jacob and Rachel in a spacious landscape. But how different from Elsheimer's! The Italian uses scenery only as a setting for the action, whereas the German, a hundred years later, diminishes the figures in importance and makes them sink back into the landscape, which now asserts itself as the main element in the composition. This completes the great change from 'figures in a landscape' to 'landscape with figures', and leaves the theme ready for further development.

Elsheimer's work has an enchanting intimacy, a quite new feeling for nature. His big trees really give shade, one can almost hear his springs bubbling, there is warmth in the play of light in his picture; birds float in the sunny air, man and nature mingle harmoniously.

The picture is mentioned for the first time in the inventory for 1722.

160

ANTON RAPHAEL MENGS (1728–1779)

SELF-PORTRAIT IN A RED CLOAK   Pastel
Gallery No. P. 167   Height 55 cm. (21⁵/₈")
                                                          Width 42 cm. (16¹/₂")

Young Mengs was an example of precociously revealed talent. His father, Ismael, who was himself a painter, had great ambitions for the boy from the very moment of his birth, and had him christened by two names which in his opinion should guarantee supremacy in art – those of Raphael, the very embodiment of greatness, and of Antonio da Correggio, the personification of charm. Were these sponsors to fulfil their promise, Anton Raphael was bound to become the greatest artist of all time.

Such was the father's reasoning. And indeed, the son attained to unusual fame during his lifetime. Growing up in the Dresden of the Winckelmann period, in the shadow of the famous collection of antiquities, the budding artist developed the concept of 'noble simplicity and quiet greatness' which made his ceiling fresco *Parnassus* in the Villa Albani in Rome a model for a whole generation of classicists.

To meet his contemporaries' need for a theory that would embody their tastes, he published his *Gedanken über die Schönheit und den Geschmack der Malerei (Thoughts on Beauty and Taste in Painting)* in 1762.

Anton Raphael Mengs' more pretentious works have long since fallen out of favour. But his portraits are still fascinating. This self-portrait, painted in 1744, when he was only sixteen, already shows astonishing qualities. Its expertise apart, it reveals a psychological insight most unusual in one so young. Very few painters have mastered the art of portrait painting at such an early age.

There is something provocative in the set of the boy's head on his shoulders. The treatment is still that of the Baroque period, but the bold eyes give indication of a new approach to art.

This pastel appears for the first time in the inventory for 1765.

162

ANTON GRAFF (1736–1813)

SELF-PORTRAIT AT THE AGE OF FIFTY-EIGHT   Canvas

Gallery No. 2167   Height 168 cm. (66$^1/_8$")

Width 105 cm. (41$^3/_8$")

The painter is seated at his easel. One hand holds his brush and palette, the other droops idly from the back of the chair on which his arm rests. He is looking over his right shoulder, so that we see him almost full-face.

What the artist has attempted here, and very skilfully achieved, is not so much self-presentation as the representation of 'being' in its essence. Lavater's work on physiognomy had become so famous that it had given fresh impetus even to portraiture.

Thus it was that Anton Graff enriched the world with a whole gallery of portraits of the intellectual leaders of Germany in the second half of the eighteenth century, such men as Lessing, Wieland and Schiller. His self-portraits are numerous, from youth to age, but they are not treated as problems in the manner of Rembrandt; Graff's approach is that of a faithful chronicler, recording what he sees. The nineteenth century's interest in history is already foreshadowed here – a steady, bourgeois approach, quite opposed to the 'artistic temperament' as it is usually understood.

This painter's life was uneventful. He was born at Winterthur in Switzerland, worked for a time at Augsburg, went to Dresden in 1766 to teach at the newly-opened Academy of Art, and remained there till he died.

The self-portrait reproduced here was painted for the exhibition at the Dresden Academy in 1795 and came into the Gallery in 1832, probably straight from Graff's heirs.

164

ANGELICA KAUFFMANN (1741–1807)
PORTRAIT OF A LADY AS A VESTAL   Canvas
Gallery No. 2181   Height 91.5 cm. (36″)
                                                    Width 71.5 cm. (28¹/₈″)

Angelica Kauffmann, Swiss by birth, lived for some time in London and settled in Rome in 1782, where she joined the circle of Goethe's friends. The poet mentions her several times in the diary which forms part of his *Italienische Reise*. The entry for 22nd July 1787 notes, for example, that 'It is extremely pleasant to look at pictures with Angelica, for she has a cultivated eye and a great understanding of technical matters.'

'Technique', 'culture' and 'the congenial'—summed up in those three words, Goethe's judgment expresses one of the maxims of classicist art-theory. Art can be learnt by mastering rules, they maintain, it is simply a matter of technique. And our mentor is antiquity, to be approached as part of our education. Thus and only thus can beauty be measured, by the standard of what is pleasing and agreeable.

Fortunately the great artists of the classical period unfailingly transcended their own theories, otherwise their work would have been dry, bloodless stuff. This applies to Angelica Kauffmann as much as to the others. She was a portrait painter of great merit, and even before she left England her art had matured to a point at which her theoretical precepts were set aside. In England she was introduced to a school of portrait painting which had not forgotten to seek out and reveal the essential personality behind the outward appearance.

This portrait of a lady as a Vestal Virgin reflects the contemporary fashion for dressing up in the style of Greece and Rome, a taste in which there was a certain cultural element. The beautiful model, her head lightly covered by a veil, leans against a pedestal and holds a lamp—an allusion to the perpetual flame that burnt in the Temple of Vesta in Rome.

A sweet dignity suffuses the composition; its human charm goes far beyond any cut-and-dried programme.

The picture is mentioned for the first time in the inventory for 1782.

166

JAN VAN EYCK (c. 1390–1441)

TRYPTICH   Panels

Gallery No. 799

Centre panel: Height 27 cm. ($10^3/_8''$)

Width 21.5 cm. ($8^3/_8''$)

Wings: Height 27.5 cm. ($10^3/_4''$)

Width 8 cm. ($3^1/_8''$)

The small, intimate pictures painted by the early Netherlandish artists seemed almost incredible to their Italian contemporaries, who were accustomed to works in the grand manner. They were amazed by the precision with which a whole microcosm was often represented on a tiny surface; while their writers never tried of exclaiming how 'lifelike' and 'true to nature' were these works, which they could not extol enough.

One of the places to which Netherlandish works of art were shipped, and through the agency of which it became known in Italy, was Naples. It was to Genoa, however, that this little tryptich of Van Eyck's found its way, if we can place reliance upon the coat of arms belonging to the Ginstiniani family that was later affixed to the frame.

The altarpiece was used for family prayers, and was handy enough to be taken on journeys. The colours have the deep, lustrous quality of jewels, and the subtly differentiated lighting adds life to the scenes.

The centre panel shows the Virgin seated on a richly-decorated throne with the Child on her knee.

On the left-hand panel we see the Archangel Michael with the artist's patron kneeling beside him, and on the right-hand panel St Catherine reading a book, with her attributes, the wheel and the sword. The outside of the closed triptych depicts the Annunciation, in grisaille.

The brushwork is so delicate that its finest touches – such as the reflection of St Catherine's face in the tiny pommel of the sword – can only be seen through a magnifying-glass.

168

An inscription was recently discovered on the lower edge of the centre panel. It runs: 'Johannes De.eyck me fecit et complevit Anno DM M'CCC'XXXVII'. als. ixh. xan' (Jan van Eyck made and completed me in the Year of the Lord 1437. As well as I can). The final words, 'als ixh xan', appear on three other paintings by Van Eyck.

This retable is first mentioned in the 1765 'Catalogue' and attributed to Dürer; it had been bought in 1696 from the E. Jabach collection in Paris as the work of Hubert van Eyck.

JOOS VAN CLEVE (*c.* 1465–1540)
THE SMALL ADORATION OF THE KINGS
Gallery No. 809

Panel
Height 110 cm. (43¹/₄")
Width 70.5 cm. (27³/₄")

The first impression is one of confusion. The Virgin sits amid fantastic ruins (a combination of pillared arcades and crumbling walls covered with thatch), with the naked Child on her lap; she is offering him an apple. Before her stand the three Wise Men. Joseph, with his hat and staff, is waiting, as usual, in the background. Everything seems over-ornamental – carved jewels, rich fabrics, embroideries and fur-trimming, gifts wrought of gold and silver. The crumpled effect of the robes adds to the general air of restlessness. Even in the further distance the eye finds nothing restful at first sight. The landscape stretches away in separate ranges of hills, peopled by numerous tiny figures. Horses are being led to water, the followers of the far-travelled Kings are bringing up camels and other beasts of burden; villages, farms and castles are scattered among feathery trees, and flocks of birds fly overhead.

The Star of Bethlehem hangs in the centre, but amid all this bustle we scarcely notice it.

Only by the skill of his composition has the painter managed to convey a sense of ultimate repose, for even the jewel-like radiance of the colours helps to break up the design.

This represents a late phase, self-conscious and no longer entirely self-confident, relying upon polished technique in a deliberate effort to recreate the freshness and innocence of an earlier period, a paradise now lost for ever.

The Italian style has been consciously adopted and adapted for this purpose. This was a time when painters were travelling south to glean what they could, whereas those of earlier generations had been rich enough to rely on their own resources.

This small *Adoration* (the Dresden Gallery also has a large *Adoration* by the same artist) first appears in the 1812 catalogue.

170

DUTCH MASTER (*c.* 1500)
THE HOLY FAMILY WITH SAINTS ANNA AND JOACHIM   Panel
Gallery No. 840   Height 65.5 cm. ($25^{3}/_{4}''$)
                                                  Width 48 cm. ($18^{7}/_{8}''$)

It was the early Dutch and Flemish painters who first discovered the snug homeliness of life indoors.

Mary sits on a bench between reassuringly solid-looking walls, cautiously holding out her naked baby towards her mother, St Anna, who is offering him a pear. Joseph and Joachim are talking together in the background. Behind them lies a room with raftered ceiling, fireplace, curtained bed and cushioned seat. Light pours in through windows filled with coats of arms in stained glass. A family idyll!

But a solemn atmosphere pervades the scene. The young mother sits bolt upright on her handsome bench, as though afraid to lean back because of the heavy crown on her head. And the two men seem to be talking in whispers, for fear of disturbing the silence.

It is evident that the human aspect of genre painting, so unusually fresh and lively in this picture, has been damped down out of respect for the sacred character of the scene.

The floor, with its coloured tiles, is considerably foreshortened. The perspective by which the spatial values are conveyed seems to be instinctive rather than calculated. But the problems are the same that confronted the Italian painters of this period. The difference is that everything here is more intimate, more subjective, more cordial than in the South.

The artist has not yet been identified, though the picture ranks high. It first appears in the inventory of the Dresden Gallery for 1753, and is described in the earliest entries as by Van Eyck or his school. In 1884 it is attributed for the first time to a Dutch painter. Since then the names of Geertgen, the Master of Alkmaar and Jacob Cornelis have been suggested, but never quite convincingly.

JOOS DE MOMPER (1564–1635)

WINTER LANDSCAPE
Gallery No. 875

Panel
Height 48.5 cm. (19")
Width 66 cm. (26")

Joos de Momper's pictures form a striking contrast to the idealized landscapes being painted in Rome about 1600. He, too, is inventive, but his scenes have none of the Arcadian softness of which his Italian contemporaries were so fond.

Momper had a predilection for strange, bare, arid rocks, stretching away into prospects so fantastic and remote that they might be on another planet.

He was undoubtedly influenced in this respect by Peter Brueghel the Elder, though Brueghel uses landscape more as a setting for his figures. Momper had no direct followers, with the possible exception of that solitary figure, Hercules Seghers, for Dutch landscape painting subsequently developed in the direction of greater realism.

Not that Momper was incapable of realistic painting; this *Winter Landscape,* for instance, is certainly based on the direct study of nature. In this respect he was the forerunner of artists such as Teniers.

Momper chooses a fairly high viewpoint, so that his eye may carry as far as possible. This was an old principle, made familiar by Patenier. Later it became the fashion to place the horizon at a lower level, so as to give a normal range of vision.

A column of peasants' carts is moving slowly along a pathway that runs through a wood. The leading horse has slipped and fallen. The driver and his wife are struggling with might and main to get it to its feet again. An old man is driving two lean pigs.

The figures in Momper's pictures were not usually painted by him, but by another painter who specialized in this kind of work.

The scene is articulated by the trees in a manner that recalls an engraving. The leafless branches converge at the top like the intricate fan-vaulting of some Gothic cathedral. A church and some farmhouse can be seen in the blue-green distance.

The picture makes its first appearance in the inventory for 1754.

174

PETER PAUL RUBENS (1577–1640)

St Jerome   Canvas

Gallery No. 955   Height 236 cm. (92$^{7}/_{8}$")
                                              Width 163.5 cm. (64$^{1}/_{4}$")

St Jerome was one of the four Fathers of the Church. He earned special merit by his revision of the Vulgate – the Latin version of the Bible. He lived for a time in the desert of Chalcis as a penitent and hermit, and later in a monastery near Bethlehem. Legend has it that while there he removed a thorn from a lion's paw, and the grateful beast afterwards followed him about like a dog.

St Jerome is sometimes portrayed as a Father of the Church, sometimes while translating the Bible in his cell, and sometimes as a pious penitent in the desert.

It is in the third of these roles that Rubens chose to depict him here.

The dignified old man, dressed only in a long, billowing red cloak, kneels in front of a stone on which a crucifix stands beside some open books and a skull. Sublimely self-reproachful, he is carrying out the penance he has laid upon himself. His inseparable companion, the lion, is sleeping peacefully at his feet.

There is something monumental about the life-size figure of the Saint, with his long, silvery beard. We sense the Italian influence to which Rubens was subjected between 1600 and 1608, chiefly in Rome. For all its outward humility, there is a forcefulness, even imperiousness, about the scene.

The picture was touched up at a later period, which accounts for the slightly arid aspect it displays in parts. But Rubens' mastery is clearly evident, particularly in the landscape background, the trees with their beautiful foliage which likewise recall certain Italian innovations of that period.

This work came to Dresden in 1746 from the ducal Gallery at Modena.

PETER PAUL RUBENS (1577–1640)
OLD WOMAN WITH A BRAZIER   Panel
Gallery No. 958   Height 116 cm. (45⁵/₈")

Height 116 cm. (45$^5/_8$")
Width 92 cm. (36$^1/_4$")

The seventeenth-century painters loved chiaroscuro. Caravaggio was the first to adopt it as a general element of composition, about the year 1600; Elsheimer showed that it could be used to convey more intimate values.

Rubens had come into contact with both these men during the time he spent in Rome. He had been asked for an expert opinion on one of Caravaggio's pictures in 1607, and he was on terms of personal friendship with Elsheimer. A letter from him to J. Faber, a doctor who had settled in Rome, expresses his grief at the untimely death of the young German artist.

It is Rembrandt's name that usually springs to mind at the mention of chiaroscuro painting. But this picture shows, among others, that Rubens, too, concerned himself with the problem, influenced by his impressions of Caravaggio and Elsheimer.

Three people are gathered round a fire in a cave – an old woman, holding the brazier, a boy who is blowing the sparks with puffed-out cheeks, and a young man gazing placidly into the flames.

The picture is built up from contrasting patches of bright light and heavy shadows, its reddish glow fading out into blue-black darkness.

This is a fragment of a large work by Rubens, now at Brussels; old copies show that it originally depicted Venus in a grotto, attended by nymphs. After the Dresden fragment had been sawn out, the patch was painted over by some other hand and the whole thing transformed into Vulcan's forge.

The first mention of this picture at Dresden occurs in Guarienti's inventory of 1753.

178

PETER PAUL RUBENS (1577–1640)

BOAR HUNT

Gallery No. 962

Panel

Height 137 cm. (53⁷/₈″)
Width 168 cm. (66¹/₈″)

The picture resounds with noise – the furious barking of the boarhounds, the blast of the horn, the rush of wind and the song of birds in the bright sky.

The hunt is not yet over. The beaters and dogs have cut off the boar's way of escape and now he stands at bay before the hunters with their lowered weapons. Elegant horsemen canter past, one of them drawing his sword to give the *coup de grâce* to the powerful beast.

The scene is a whirl of movement. The muscular hounds are struggling desperately to outstrip one another, panting as they try to scramble over the branches of a fallen tree, amongst which the boar has taken refuge.

Jacob Burckhardt says that this 'glorious woodland light' conveys a 'moral', a sense of 'the inevitability of destiny'. The magnificent trees seem to participate in what is going on below them. Their mighty trunks twist in spirals, their spreading branches sway, their tall crests sweep upward to proclaim that man, beast and plant are animated by the same breath of life.

The work is imbued, even to its smallest and most inconspicuous detail, with a vital tension that only a spirit as great as that of Rubens could maintain.

This picture came to Dresden in 1749 from the imperial gallery at Prague.

180

PETER PAUL RUBENS (1577–1640)

BATHSHEBA

Gallery No. 965

Panel

Height 175 cm. (68$^7/_8$")
Width 126 cm. (49$^5/_8$")

King David had seen Bathsheba, wife of Uriah, while she was bathing, and had fallen immediately and violently in love with her. Regardless of the sin he was committing, he sent a messenger to summon her.

Bathsheba was often shown in pictures, for she gave painters an opportunity of portraying a woman's beauty unhindered.

The subject was particularly calculated to appeal to Rubens.

This Dresden picture belongs to his late, mature period. He has painted Bathsheba in the likeness of his young second wife, Hélène Fourment, whom he married after the death of Isabella Brandt, and this adds an intimate, personal charm to the work.

The young beauty, conscious of her loveliness but with nothing of the coquette about her, is to be seen in her shift; a fur cloak has fallen from her shoulders to reveal her glowing limbs; she toys with a string of pearls while her golden hair falls in a wave over the arm of the maidservant who is dressing it. It is almost with an air of expectancy that she turns towards the Negro boy as he hurries up to her with King David's letter, greeted by the excited yapping of her little dog. In the distance we sense rather than see King David, looking out from the parapet of his lofty palace.

All this is suffused with marvellous colour, ursurpassed for its magnificence, its shimmering radiance and its transparency. No material obstacle whatsoever seems to check the artist's imagination.

This picture was acquired for the Dresden Gallery through Le Leu in Paris in 1749.

182

DAVID TENIERS THE YOUNGER
(1610–1690)   Canvas
FLEMISH KERMESSE WITH COUPLE DANCING
Gallery No. 1083   Height 142 cm. (55⁷/₈″)
                        Width 178 cm. (70¹/₈″)

A cheerful, bustling scene. The local peasants
are eating and drinking at long tables set out
in front of the village inn. The first pair of
dancers is revolving to the strains of a fiddle
and a bass-viol, while others crowd round to
watch. Drink is flowing liberally. A cellar-
man is filling jugs from a cask.

Peter Brueghel had preceded Teniers as a
painter of country festivities, but in his pictures there is always some hint of a symbolical
intention, which is entirely lacking in the later
artist, whose sole aim is to depict the actual
life of the peasants in realistic detail.

Teniers had great success in his own lifetime,
amassed wealth, acquired a country seat, and
became Court painter to the Archduke Leopold
William, who made him director of his gallery
and finally raised him to the nobility. So it is
not surprising that his personality does not
come out very strongly in his work. One feels
that his heart was never 'in it' to the same
extent as Adriaen Brouwer's or Van Ostade's.

Teniers looks at the merry-making of country
folk with the condescending eye of a spectator
from the world of fashion, and it is in that
spirit that he has depicted this village fair. In
the background of the picture is a landscape
with a manor-house from which the squire
and his lady have just emerged to enjoy the
spectacle of the jollifications from a seemly
distance. A servant is hurrying up with a trayful of drinks to refresh
the gentry.

Tenier's colours are sappy and he lays them on with a flourish. Here
again we find a difference between Flemish painting and Dutch, the

184

latter being on the whole graver, more restrained and more strongly accented.

This picture was bought in 1746, through Le Leu, from the Araignon collection in Paris.

FRANS SNYDERS (1579–1657)

STILL-LIFE WITH A LADY AND A PARROT   Canvas
Gallery No. 1191   Height 154 cm. (60⅝")
                                                       Width 237 cm. (93¼")

The Dutch were given to painting small pictures in which everyday life was realistically and unpretentiously recorded, whereas the Flemish painters were more interested in the fashionable world. With them, the quiet relationship between the observer and the objects around him is replaced by a love of display and pomp. The difference extends even to still-life paintings.

Frans Snyders, a collaborator of Rubens, was partial to large canvases into which he could pack a vast quantity of fruit, vegetables, marine creatures, game and poultry. He was also fond of including in his still-life paintings either a human figure, such as a kitchenmaid or a huntsman, or some domestic animal, a cat or dog, which is seen licking the blood of the freshly killed game. Here we see fashionably dressed young woman holding a parrot—an exotic bird brought home, perhaps, by some seafarer from a distant land. The artist is delighted to include this strange creature in his painting.

Snyders's work is always suptuous and showy. Everything that house and garden can supply is laid out as if for exhibition. There is something old-fashioned about it all, reminiscent of the kitchen and market pictures of artists such as Pieter Aertsen. This type of still-life is well on the way to genre painting.

The colours, too, are splendid; the general background is a deep grey-green, an admirable foil to the bright plumage of a game-bird or the vivid red of a lobster's shell.

It is easy to imagine what a gay, decorative effect such pictures must have produced on the walls of royal residences.

This work was bought for the Dresden Gallery in 1743, in Paris.

186

ADRIAEN BROUWER (1605–1638)
PEASANTS FALLING OUT OVER A GAME OF CARDS
Gallery No. 1059

Panel
Height 26.5 cm. (10³/₈")
Width 34.5 cm. (13¹/₂")

What an uproar! Three peasants are brawling round an upturned barrel; they had been playing cards – apparently without too much regard for honesty. One of them has jumped to his feet, seized his neighbour by the hair, deaf to the man's wailing protestations of innocence, and is swinging an earthenware jug down on his head. The third member of the party is drawing his knife, ready for all eventualities. In the dimly-lit background of the room two old men are sitting by the fireside, watching the brawlers with a mixture of anxiety and annoyance.

Cheating at cards had been a favourite subject for painters since the time of Caravaggio and his school. Valentin de Boulogne invests his version with tremendous tension, while treating it with a kind of studied restraint – the whole thing seems to be happening almost surreptitiously, so that the man who has been swindled is hardly aware of how it came about. Brouwer's approach is much more forthright. What he relishes is unmitigated boorishness, and he portrays it ruthlessly.

But the skilful composition is in striking contrast to the uncouth subject; it is here that the artist reveals his mastery. By grouping his figures in a triangle he succeeds in making their violent movements agreeable to the eye without any loss of dynamic vigour.

The colours are wonderful; one feels that they could be carried on in broad brush-strokes beyond the limits of the small picture. A bright bottle-green harmonizes well with earthy brown tones.

Brouwer stands midway between the Dutch and Flemish schools. He began as a pupil of Frans Hals and later settled permanently at Antwerp, where he worked hard and prospered.

The picture is mentioned for the first time in the 1817 catalogue.

ANTHONY VAN DYCK (1599–1641)

PORTRAIT OF A LADY IN BLACK   Canvas

Gallery No. 1028   Height 126 cm. (49⅝")

Width 92 cm. (36¼")

Van Dyck was one of the most sought-after portrait painters of his day. This does not mean to say that he was one of the most profound, but it is unfair to dismiss his work as merely agreeable and technically skilful routine. Like Rosalba Carriera and other successful artists, he was often confronted by sitters whose features were depressingly insignificant. It is fascinating to see how all his portraits manage to compensate for this by the air of distinction he lends to his models.

The Dresden Gallery possesses a number of portraits, painted at different periods of Van Dyck's career, all possessing qualities of style, grace and spirit which show what the could make out of even the most unpromising material.

Van Dyck was a precocious genius, working in Rubens' studio when only seventeen years old; he then went to Genoa, where he was overwhelmed with commissions for portraits; and from 1632 onwards he was in London as Court painter. His influence long outlasted him, and the English portrait painters of the eighteenth century, in particular, drew much of their inspiration from him.

This *Portrait of a Lady in Black* (which has a *Portrait of a Gentleman* as its companion-piece) belongs to his later period.

The style of painting is relaxed, and the colour scheme preponderantly dark. The background, where a little landscape scene is hinted at rather than defined, is painted with the oblique, flaky brushwork of which Gainsborough was a later exponent.

These portraits were no doubt excellent likenesses. And a likeness that manages to be slightly flattering is always a great attraction for sitters. Rembrandt used to offend his models by paying more attention to personality than to type.

The *Portrait of a Lady in Black* and its companion piece were bought for the Dresden Gallery in 1741 by Gallery Inspector Heinecken at Hamburg.

190

ANTHONY VAN DYCK (1599–1641)

PORTRAIT OF A MAN IN ARMOUR WITH A RED ARMBAND   Canvas
Gallery No. 1026   Height 90 cm. $(33^{3}/_{8}'')$
                                                        Width 70 cm. $(27^{5}/_{8}'')$

It is hard to believe that Van Dyck's young man in armour is a real soldier, fit for the hurly-burly of a trooper's life in the Thirty Years War. With his rather pensive features and sensitive hand, he looks more like an artist who has put on the heavy armour as a kind of fancy dress. Even the lively turn of the head seems to be a superficial gesture rather than prompted by genuine interest.

Rembrandt too was fond of painting men in armour, but with him the 'fancy dress' is approached from a completely different standpoint. Despite his partiality for magnificent, costly 'props', the metallic glint of a neck-piece or the hard lines of a helmet are merely, for him, the occasion for rendering the play of light which endows a picture with shimmering depths. Never are costume, ornament, weapons or armour used to bring out the psychology of the model.

With Van Dyck it is just the opposite. What gives life to his *Portrait of a Man in Armour* is the dissimilarity of the man and his dress. To put it another way, the personality of the sitter is deliberately brought out by the contrast between his long, wavy hair and the hard iron of the armour.

For all its restraint, the black and grey colour scheme is used to rich and ingenious effect. The brushwork looks quite effortless, but in reality it is carefully studied and laid on with the utmost skill.

The picture came to Dresden in 1741 from the Wallenstein collection at Dux.

192

ANTHONY VAN DYCK (1599–1641)

DRUNKEN SILENUS

Gallery No. 1017

Canvas

Height 107 cm. (42^1/$_8$")

Width 91.5 cm. (34")

The aged, drunken Silenus, his vine-wreathed head sunk on this wrinkled breast, is stumbling along, supported on either side by helpful companions. Behind them, a dark-skinned man among his following is passing his tongue thirstily over his lips, while another is emptying a jug in eager gulps.

This theme was familiar to Van Dyck from his days in Rubens' workshop, and the spirit of his great master breathes through the whole picture. But details of the composition reveal the independent young artist.

Mythical depths always underly Rubens' work, for all its sensuality, whereas Van Dyck turns everything to witty refinement. The difference is apparent in the sensitive play of the exaggeratedly long fingers. The way in which the woman's soft arm encircles the old man's slack, dangling hand is particularly striking. Rubens' touch, however delicate, would have treated this with more firmness.

The colour and brushwork are admirable. The interplay of light and shadow is almost liquid. A silvery bloom overlays the warm red and glowing blue of the clothing and sublimates the daring theme. The master's sensitive touch seems to vibrate through every detail of the picture.

The first mention of this painting occurs in the inventory for 1722.

194

FRANS HALS THE ELDER (c. 1580–1666)

PORTRAIT OF A YOUNG MAN IN A YELLOW AND GREY COAT   Panel

Gallery No. 1358   Height 24.5 cm. (9⅝″)

Width 19.5 cm. (7⅜″)

Anyone who knew this Dresden picture by Frans Hals only from reproductions would be surprised at the small size of the original, which measures hardly more than two hand-breadths. Yet to the mind's eye it seems, as only a really great work of art can do, to take on substantial dimensions.

The young model, with his slouch hat and beautiful lace collar leans slightly backwards and gazes out at the world with an air of bold self-assurance.

The spontaneous, direct vitality of Frans Hals' portraits is enough in itself to win our sympathy. He does not go in for psychological romances; he is quite satisfied to record what he sees before his eyes.

The manner is as straightforward as the matter. No complicated, time-wasting technical experiments; the whole thing comes straight off the brush as it moves animatedly but unerringly to and fro.

The Impressionist painters of the late nineteenth century were naturally fascinated by Hals, in whom they found their own ideas foreshadowed and endorsed. Max Liebermann, in particular, had a great admiration for him.

Frans Hals lived very long, but though his genius brought him full command of his medium he did not develop any distinctive manner in his old age. Not given to brooding over problems, he had nothing of Rembrandt's introspective nature.

Houbraken relates a host of characteristic anecdotes about Frans Hals, which suggest that he must have been a popular figure. He died in the poorhouse at Haarlem, a town which now has its own Frans Hals museum.

This picture, with another of the same format, was bought for Dresden from the Wallenstein collection at Dux in 1741.

196

JAN VAN GOYEN (1596–1656)

SUMMER ON THE RIVER

Gallery No. 1338 C

Oval panel

Height 68 cm. (26³/₄")

Width 90.5 cm. (33¹/₂")

Jan van Goyen was born at Leyden. He travelled all over his native Holland, sketchbook in hand, before settling at The Hague to transform his notes into paintings.

His vast output provides the most faithful record of that flat landscape, spanned by high-arching skies.

Goyen used a restricted palette. In this picture the illusion of diffused sunlight is created by yellow-brown tints with a golden sheen. Boats enliven the wide, smooth expanse of the river. In the foreground, some fishermen are hauling in their nets. The stream flows between low banks. A tree in full leaf forms the central point of the composition. Wagons are assembled outside the farmhouse on the right. In the distance, on the further bank, lies a village whose church spire thrusts up into a sky dappled with drifting clouds.

This is a typical 'Dutch' picture inasmuch as it can safely be said to reflect the outlook of several generations of the public. Even nowadays, anyone contemplating a Dutch landscape will be involuntarily reminded of some painting by Van Goyen.

The picture is signed with the painter's monogram and dated 1643. It first appeared in the 1817 catalogue.

198

WILLEM CLAESZ HEDA (1594–1680/82)
BREAKFAST TABLE WITH BLACKBERRY PIE   Panel
Gallery No. 1371   Height 54 cm. (21¼")
                                                             Width 82 cm. (32¼")

It was Houbraken (1630–1719), the Dutch writer on art, who coined the
term *'stilleven'* for pictures of inanimate objects such as fruit, flowers or
the implements of everyday life; it passed into English terminology as
'still-life' and into French as *'nature morte'*.

The history of the still-life followed the same course as that of landscape – in other words, from a subordinate or extraneous position in the
composition it gradually expanded until it filled the whole picture.

This development culminated in seventeenth-century Holland, when a
number of artists made a speciality of still-life painting; it had a special
appeal for Dutch painters, with their fondness for lingering, for passivity.

This particular work has three outstanding qualities. First we are delighted by the mastery with which Heda portrays the texture of his objects, making them almost tangible – the metallic glint of the beautifully
chased goblet, the cool gleam of wine in the glasses, and the juicy-looking
pie. Secondly, we admire the way in which this casual grouping of lifeless
objects has built up something that is 'alive', how the placing of every
item is so exactly right.

And finally we are led to reflect on the 'vanitas' motif, which is evoked
by the overturned glass with its broken rim and reinforced by the richly
decorated pocket-watch which in itself would seem slightly out of place
on a breakfast table.

So it is that in this still-life the artist has far transcended the mechanical
depiction of inanimate objects.

The picture is signed and bears the date 1631. It was bought for the
Gallery from an Amsterdam art dealer in 1857.

SALOMON KONINCK (1609–1656)
THE HERMIT
Gallery No. 1589

Canvas
Height 121 cm. (47^5/$_8$")
Width 93.5 cm. (36^1/$_2$")

During the Italian Renaissance, portraits of learned men came into favour as successors to the busts of philosophers created by sculptors in classical times. But this widely popular practice was not merely the revival of an ancient tradition, it reflected the interest in learning which was a basic trait of the Renaissance and which left its mark on every form of artistic creation.

Mathematics, anatomy and nature study found their way into art with perspective, nude studies, and landscape painting. From this it was a natural step to depict the scholar himself, deep in his books or working with mathematical instruments.

Even pictures of the saints reveal this trend. A suitable and favourite theme was that of St Jerome in his study; here we think in particular of Albrecht Dürer, but the subject was also handled, in engravings or paintings, by Jan van Eyck, Botticelli, Ghirlandaio and others.

The seventeenth century carried the process further. This, indeed, was the period in which science, in the modern sense, really came to birth – the period of Descartes, who published his *Discours de la méthode* in 1637.

But the anecdotal style, in which the serious treatment accorded to the problems of painting by artists of earlier generations was lightened – to a greater or less extent, at the painter's choice – by the introduction of a pleasing element of 'genre', was also popular, especially in Holland.

Salomon Koninck's *Hermit* is a charming example of this. His old man, with the wrinkled face and long, silky beard, is neither a real scholar (they were in the universities) nor a real saint (they had gone out with the Middle Ages), but a hermit – in other words, an eccentric who has taken to solitude in order to pursue his edifying studies undisturbed.

Salomon Koninck was much influenced by Rembrandt; such a picture as this could never have been painted if the great Dutch master had not created his impressive heads of old men.

The work is dated 1643 and first appears in the inventory for 1722.

202

GERARD DOU (1613–1675)
THE OLD SCHOOLMASTER   Panel
Gallery No. 1709   Height 32 cm. (12⅝")
                                                    Width 24.5 cm. (9¾")

Gerard Dou evolved a delicately meticulous style of painting which won him many admirers among his contemporaries. Influential agents took options on pictures by him before they were finished, to make sure of being able to meet their clients' orders. King Charles I owned works by him, so did Archduke Leopold Wilhelm of Austria. Even the Uffizi in Florence commissioned a self-portrait for its famous portrait collection.

The artist based his prices on matter-of-fact business considerations, charging one 'Flemish pound' per hour of work.

His pictures, most of them small, are painted with such care that the individual brush-strokes are invisible to the naked eye and can be seen only through a magnifying glass such as he himself used when painting them. Dou's own good opinion of his works may be gathered from the fact that he used to keep them in chests, away from dust and light; he decorated the lids of some of these chests with still-life pictures.

Dou has special importance as head of the Leyden School of Painting, which he founded. He chose scenes of everyday middle-class life as his subjects and his pictures served as an example and encouragement to a whole generation of genre painters.

He himself was trained in Rembrandt's workshop at Leyden, between 1628 and 1631, and in his early work he was completely under the influence of his great compatriot, who was also the inspiration for the chiaroscuro used by Dou in many paintings, even in later life.

Dou is fond of setting his genre scenes in a framework of masonry, or in an alcove from which a curtain has been drawn back.

The Dresden schoolmaster is shown in this way, depicted with almost pedantic exactitude in the act of cleaning his quill pen. A document with a red seal, an hour-glass, a birdcage and the spectacles on the old man's nose – it is details such as these that have long been the picture's chief attraction.

It is signed and dated 1671, and first appears in the 1817 catalogue.

204

REMBRANDT (1606–1669)
GANYMEDE CAUGHT UP BY THE EAGLE   Canvas
Gallery No. 1558   Height 171 cm. (67³/₈")
                                                        Width 130 cm. (51¹/₈")

Ganymede was the son of King Tros, after whom Troy was named. His celebrated beauty aroused the passion of Zeus. Legend relates that the Father of the Gods, in the form of an eagle, swooped down on the Trojan plain and carried off the boy to serve as his cup-bearer.

The theme was popular with artists, especially with the Italian Baroque painters; it enabled them to gratify the prevailing worship of beauty and to grapple with the problem of representing complex movements in artistic form.

The model used by Annibale Carracci for his picture of Fame, likewise now at Dresden, would also have made an ideal Ganymede.

Rembrandt's idea of depicting the favourite of the Gods as an ugly, loudly wailing and extremely human little boy seems a kind of defiance, after so much nobility.

In point of fact, Rembrandt tended to be unconventional in his attitude towards the antique. On more than one occasion he handled a mythological scene in a farcical manner. His Rape of Proserpina, now at Berlin, is a kind of tussle. But he never descended to vulgarity.

His Ganymede scene, for all its uncompromising bluntness, has more in it than meets the eye at first glance. There is something ominous, menacing, about the huge, heavy bird as it grasps the desperately struggling boy by his shirt. The light glares pitilessly down on the little naked body. The utter helplessness of the victim robs the situation of any element of comedy, as the bird of prey rises on heavy, silent pinions into the lowering heavens. There is nothing to suggest that love has prompted this scene, nothing to help us visualize the Olympian paradise where Ganymede is to serve his lord with wine in richly-chased bowls.

This work was painted during Rembrandt's early Amsterdam period; it is signed in full and bears the date 1635. It was bought for the Dresden Gallery by Heinecken at Hamburg in 1751.

REMBRANDT (1606–1669)
SELF-PORTRAIT WITH SASKIA
Gallery No. 1559

Canvas
Height 161 cm. (63³/₈")
Width 111 cm. (43³/₄")

This picture is a burst of high spirits. It belongs to the tradition of Dutch tavern paintings, which dealt with a specific and often very rough milieu.

Here again, despite the merry mood, there is something aggressive, defiant, in the attitude of the young bridegroom as he sits with his beautiful, pampered bride on his knee – as though the miller's son from Leyden is wanting to prove that he can defy convention.

The picture was painted about 1635, only three years after Rembrandt had settled in Amsterdam. In 1634 he had married Saskia van Uylenburgh, the daughter of a wealthy and respected family, and he had just achieved his first successes as a portrait painter. Surely so much good luck was enough to justify him in raising his glass to toast the spectator, outside the picture!

The colours are gay and brilliant, a harmony of green, red and golden brown. The picture has obvious faults of composition and anatomy: Saskia is so disproportioned that, as an early critic remarked, she had better not try to stand up. But it is these very weaknesses which demonstrate the folly of measuring genius by pedantic standards. A poem should be read and understood at a glance, not spelt out in syllables, and a work of art is always greater than the sum of its component features. Only in minor works are faults disturbingly apparent; the grand manner dwarfs them into insignificance. So this self-portrait by Rembrandt has a perfect right to its position among the most popular and fascinating works in the Dresden Gallery, for which it was bought in 1751 through Le Leu, in Paris.

208

REMBRANDT (1606–1669)

THE BITTEN-HUNTER
Gallery No. 1561

Panel

Height 121 cm. (47⅝″)
Width 89 cm. (35″)

In this painting Rembrandt combines three pictures in one – the sporting subject, the still-life and the portrait. It adds up to a testimony and a piece of autobiography.

Rembrandt is almost unique among painters in the persistence with which, from youth to old age, he pursued the quest for his own innermost being. His efforts to capture it are recorded in a host of self-portraits – paintings, drawings, engravings – which, taken in chronological order, vividly illustrate his growing stature.

He was never a gossip, like so many painters of his day. But neither was he wrapped in silence, like Vermeer. What he communicated was of philosophical tenor. His portraits, including those of himself, are anthropology in visual form. Looking at them – at all these monologues – we come to realize that in point of fact they are dialogues, that they have a certain bipolarity, depending as they do upon the analysis of the ego in all its multitudinous aspects. The operation is directed by the subject himself, by means of searching glances into the mirror. This may perhaps even explain Rembrandt's propensity for changing his appearance by theatrical disguises.

In this picture he is dressed as a hunter. But he keeps himself in the background. Guided by the light, our attention is arrested by the dead bird, whose soft plumage is wonderfully drawn and asserts itself independently as a kind of still-life.

Comparing this work with the self-portrait with Saskia, painted four years earlier, we are struck by its air of pensive reserve. Pride of place is given to physical beauty, whether in life or in death. The thought of the transitory nature of all earthly things may be present too. Grief seems to cast a shadow over this self-portrait.

The work is signed and bears the date 1639. It first appears in what is known as the Guarienti inventory.

210

REMBRANDT (1606–1669)
SASKIA WITH A RED ROSE   Panel
Gallery No. 1562   Height 98.5 cm. $(38^{3}/_{4}'')$
                                             Width 82.5 cm. $(32^{1}/_{4}'')$

Saskia with a Red Rose was painted in 1641. Rembrandt's son, Titus, was christened on 22nd September of that year, and less than ten months later, on 14th July 1642, Saskia died.

This Dresden portrait is the last that Rembrandt painted of his wife before her death. There is, indeed, another, dated 1643, now in Berlin, but even if Saskia actually sat for it, it was not finished while she was alive.

Saskia with a Red Rose is the most tranquil picture Rembrandt ever painted of his beloved wife. She was carrying Titus in her womb; she intimates this with a cautious gesture of her left hand, and her right hand holds the flower from which the work takes its name.

The atmosphere has such intimacy that comment is silenced. The relationship between the painter and his model is so intensely personal that outsiders shrink from trespassing upon it.

The colours chosen by Rembrandt are full to satiety, almost solemn, with a richness worthy of the cherished sitter. They are laid on with countless touches of the brush, ranging from the thinnest of layers to a paste-like relief. A warm, soft red, emerging from darkness, provides the over-all tone of the picture. There is the pale gleam of pearls round Saskia's neck.

The composition is based on a drawing now in the Munich collection.

This picture was bought for Dresden in 1742 from the Araignon collection in Paris.

212

REMBRANDT (1606–1669)

Portrait of a Man with Pearls on his Hat   Canvas
Gallery No. 1570   Height 82 cm. (32¼")
        Width 71 cm. (28")

Every period has its own attitude towards the different ages of man. There are times when the passing years ignored and the whole emphasis is laid on youth. Age is deemed to be something negative and even the old feel compelled to behave like young people.

At other times the contrary is true, and a dignified, patriarchal bearing is regarded as the ideal, so that even adolescents adopt the dress, hairstyle and mannerisms they hope will make them look much older than they are.

It is more logical, but more difficult, to accept every age as it really is. And one of the primary characteristics of great art is to give dignity to age, however great the love of youth.

Rembrandt succeeded admirably in this. He painted people at all times of life, showing them all with the values appropriate to their particular stage of development. His numerous portraits of old men are particularly instructive. Many of his models are bent and shrunken, with wrinkled, sagging cheeks, worn hands and sunken eyes. But their faces are never expressionless, dull or empty. Secret forces are still at work within – wisdom, pious trust or sturdy attachment to life. In all these men there is a breath of the sacred fire, and we revere them for it.

Sometimes a picture shows the gleam of a rich jewel, a gold brooch fastening a garment, a gold ring on a finger. There is no ostentation in this; it seems rather to hint at the inner treasures accumulated during a lifetime of experience – as in the case of this old man with the pearl-trimmed hat, a work of Rembrandt's later period. Its original impact has not been blunted by the thick crusts of over-painting.

This picture first appears in the inventory for 1722.

214

REMBRANDT (1606–1669)

SAMSON'S WEDDING   Canvas
Gallery No. 1560   Height 126 cm. (49⅝")
                   Width 175 cm. (68⅞")

When Rembrandt was in his thirties he took up the Samson theme on several occasions. This was the period of his marriage to Saskia, so it is curious to note the menacing atmosphere of one of the pictures, *Samson threatening his Father-in-law, who is keeping his Wife from him,* painted in 1635 and now in Berlin.

In 1636 came *The Blinding of Samson,* now in the Städel Art Institute at Frankfort-on-Main, and in 1638 this Dresden wedding picture.

All representations of banquets in the graphic arts can ultimately be traced back to the pictures of the Last Supper, the earliest of which are the mosaic in S. Apollinare Nuovo at Ravenna and the miniature in the Codex Rossanensis (sixth century). The version painted by Leonardo da Vinci in 1497 in the refectory of Santa Maria delle Grazie, at Milan, became world-famous. Sketches made by Rembrandt show that he knew it and used it as a subject for creative study.

Here Rembrandt has broken away from Leonardo's classical, balanced symmetry and placed the centre of gravity of his composition well to the right, where Samson is seen putting the riddle to his guests. The bride, like some enthroned statue, sits with a secret, inscrutable smile on her lips, a little off-centre, and the other guests are seated round the table to the left. There is a kind of sultry voluptuousness about this feast, yet it is somehow mysterious as well. The contrasting groups – the self-absorbed couples and the men listening keenly to Samson – form an exciting contrast to Delilah in her aloofness.

216

The colour-scheme is one of muted green, russet, golden yellow and black, which seems to deaden every sound. The whole painting has a dream-like quality. The brushwork has the meticulous precision characteristic of Rembrandt at this period of his life.

The first mention of this picture occurs in the inventory for 1722.

ADRIAEN VAN OSTADE (1610–1684)
THE PAINTER IN HIS STUDIO   Panel
Gallery No. 1397   Height 38 cm. (15")
                                                             Width 35.5 cm. (14")

A rather untidy studio, but it no doubt shows us just what a painter's
workshop of that period did look like.

The painter is absorbed in his task; his right arm propped on the maul-
stick, he is working with a fine-pointed brush. A sketch is at hand to
refresh his memory, for this was long before it became the accepted thing
for artists to paint direct from nature.

Light falls softly through the leaded panes of a big window and plays
over the scene, which resembles a still-life. The picturesque chairoscuro of
the background; where an assistant is busy with his tools, is obviously
influenced by Rembrandt.

Van Ostade, a pupil of Frans Hals, lived at Haarlem and specialized in
scenes of peasant life. His *Painter in his Studio* is perfectly in keeping
with that milieu. Vermeer's studio, familiar to us from the picture in Vienna,
looks more sophisticated, more civilized, but we feel it has been somewhat
idealized for the occasion. Van Ostade is more successful in recreating the
atmosphere of a real place of work.

The picture is signed, and dated 1663. For a time it was in the Crozat
collection in Paris, where Watteau may have seen it. From there it passed
to the de la Bouexière collection and thence, through Le Leu, to Dresden
in 1754.

218

FERDINAND BOL (1616–1680)

JACOB'S DREAM   Canvas
Gallery No. 1604   Height 128 cm. (50³/₈")
                                                    Width 97 cm. (38¹/₈")

Jacob, after obtaining the blessing of his father Isaac, had to take to flight
because he had induced his elder twin brother, Esau, to exchange his
birthright for a mess of pottage. The journey was to end in his meeting with
Rachel, his future wife, at the well – the theme chosen by Palma Vecchio
for his magnificent picture in the Dresden Gallery.

The Old Testament relates (Genesis, Chap. 28) how Jacob lay down one
night to sleep by the wayside and had a wonderful dream, in which he saw
a ladder reaching up to heaven, and angels ascending and descending, while
God's voice from on high pronounced a blessing on him.

Ferdinand Bol has taken this as the subject of his picture, but he has made
something quite individual out of it. The central feature of the painting is a
blaze of light, about which the Bible says nothing at all. Radiance pours
down in a golden flood out of the dark sky, bathing the sleeper as he lies
beside the path, reclining against a green mound. A strange, exaggeratedly
tall and slender angel in a white robe stands with right hand extended above
the dreaming man. Other angels are seen in the flood of light which suffuses
the whole scene described in the Bible. The picture glows with colour,
graduating from the deepest darkness to the bright glow above, and with
something of a rainbow's iridescence in the wings of the standing angel.

In this work Ferdinand Bol comes near to equalling his master, Rembrandt, especially in the idea of taking the heavenly radiance as the central
feature of the painting.

The work is first mentioned in the inventory for 1722.

220

ISAAC VAN OSTADE (1621–1649)
GAMES ON THE ICE   Panel
Gallery No. 1491   Height 33.5 cm. (25$^1/_8$")
                                                        Width 40 cm. (27$^3/_4$")

Isaac van Ostade was the pupil of his brother Adriaen and, like him, a genre painter with a partiality for themes illustrating life on the roads and outside taverns.

His winter scenes have great charm. They prove that landscape painting, first developed in rather idealized form in Rome about 1600, had by now been extended to include realism. Artists had gone out to study the changing aspects of the countryside at different hours of the day and seasons of the year.

The Dutch and Flemish painters could look back to Brueghel as their forerunner in this respect, though his pictures of the seasons are still in the nature of calendar illustrations. For Isaac van Ostade that approach was completely outmoded. What interested him was the portrayal of scenes from daily life, landscape being used like a stage setting.

Holland, with its network of canals, provided in those days, and indeed still does, ideal opportunities for skating and sleigh-riding whenever frost transformed its waterways into sheets of ice.

Here, then, we see muffled-up figures making the most of it. A man with a load of faggots pauses to chat.

There is a cheerful simplicity about the whole work. The even, silver-grey tone of the landscape contributes to the mood. The further reaches are veiled in chilly mist, with a suggestion of rime in the air.

This little picture came to Dresden in 1754 from the de la Bouexière collection in Paris.

222

GABRIEL METSU (1629–1667)
PORTRAIT OF THE ARTIST WITH HIS WIFE   Panel
Gallery No. 1732   Height 35.5 cm. ($13^1/_8$")
                                                            Width 30.5 cm. (12")

This double portrait, only recently identified as representing the artist and his wife, has a certain resemblance to Rembrandt's famous portrait of himself and Saskia. Both couples are seen at table, and in each case the artist is sitting with his arm round his wife and his free hand gaily holding up a glass.

But Rembrandt's picture is altogether more high-spirited, more aggressively festive; Metsu treats the subject more as a genre painting, on a much smaller scale, and his figures are rather doll-like, as though arranged for a *tableau vivant*.

There are a number of pleasing features – such as the innkeeper's wife, chalking up the customers' scores on a board in the background – which show that the artist was a keen observer of his everyday surroundings.

On the brightly polished table lies a still-life composition – fish, bread and a jug of wine.

Painting and colour reach the highest degree of perfection, with several touches of bright colour to enliven the scene.

The picture is signed, and dated 1661. According to the inventory for 1722, it came into the *Kunstkammer* in 1720.

224

JAN STEEN (1626–1679

MOTHER AND CHILD   Canvas on panel
Gallery No. 1726   Height 29 cm. (11³/₈")
                                                       Width 24.5 cm. (9³/₄")

The time-honoured theme of the mother and child, which was consecrated
by its early adoption in Christian art, is handled by Jan Steen in an
entrancingly natural manner.

The Italian artists of the fifteenth and sixteenth centuries had shown an
increasing tendency to make their Madonna pictures more secular and
'human', and the Dutch seventeenth-century painters seem to have altogether discarded the element of ambivalence.

The young mother we see in Steen's picture, sitting casually at the open
window, is nothing more than a pretty peasant woman, feeding her baby
with pap from a basin. The sturdy, chubby-cheeked infant in her lap is
thickly wrapped in swaddling-clothes.

And yet the composition retains a suggestion of the old 'Virgin and Child'
formula developed by the Italian Renaissance, even to the glimpse of landscape in the background, seen through the window. This may account for
the air of majesty that somehow emanates from the scene, despite its
unassuming, commonplace aspect.

Jan Steen was a many-sided artist, one of the most versatile painters of
his day, with exceptionally prolific ideas. A brewer and innkeeper, he had
ample opportunity to observe and study the aspects of life that appealed to
his native sense of humour. This picture of the mother with her child shows
a quieter, more pensive side of his character.

The work is mentioned for the first time in the inventory for 1722.

JACOB VAN RUISDAEL (1628/9–1682)
THE JEWISH CEMETERY   Canvas
Gallery No. 1502   Height 84 cm. (33$^1/_8$")
                                                    Width 95 cm. (37$^3/_8$")

Heavy clouds lower in the sky. A brook flows and eddies through an
abandoned graveyard, beneath thick, gloomy-looking trees. There is no sign
of life. Cold light bathes the scene.

An unusual idea for a picture!

Jacob van Ruisdael stands somewhat apart from the other landscape
painters of his day. He resembles his Dutch contemporaries inasmuch as his
work is based on the direct observation of nature. What distinguishes him
is his approach to his themes, which gives the first indication of what might
be called a natural philosophy. This picture of the Jewish burialground is
pervaded by one idea – the perishableness of all earthly things. Trees grow
tall, wither, fall and rot. Men die; they try to perpetuate their memory by
erecting massive tombstones in graveyards, but the monuments collapse,
sapped from below by the rushing waters of the stream, which proves
stronger than they. The theme is evoked again by the ruins of the building
in the background.

This is a dark *memento mori,* a cry of *'Vanitas vanitatem';* it acts as a foil
to the sensual delight of Baroque art, giving it deeper and more ominous
implications.

The symbolic values underlying many of Ruisdael's landscapes were to
fascinate a number of early-nineteenth-century artists, especially the German
romantic painters Carl Gustav Carus – who, like Ruisdael, was a doctor –
and Caspar David Friedrich.

Goethe, who often visited the Dresden Gallery, also wrote a penetrating
essay on the landscape paintings of this great Dutchman.

Dresden possesses eleven attested works by Ruisdael. This one is first
mentioned in the inventory for 1754.

228

JAN VERMEER VAN DELFT (1632–1675)

GIRL READING A LETTER

Gallery No. 1336

Canvas

Height 83 cm. (32⅝")
Width 64.5 cm. (25½")

There is something of the still-life about every picture by Vermeer. In this one it is the dish of fruit that provides the touch of *nature-morte*. This avoids any relationship between the girl and the spectator. We feel that the curtain in front of the painting has only just been drawn back, and will fall again in a moment, to hide the scene.

There is no escape into the open, even through the window; looking out of it, we are brought up short by a blank wall. But that window admits the light which is really what brings the picture to life.

The Impressionists were the first to make a systematic attempt to transform light into colour and create a universe out of colours. In Vermeer's day this was a hazardous undertaking, and only he ventured upon it. In this painting he uses a technique we often find him adopting later on. The whole picture is a mass of minute, bead-like specks of colour. We can see this best in the girl's arm, the rug, and the Delft bowl that contains the fruit. A microcosm built up from light! Unfortunately the original colour-scheme has altered a little in the course of three hundred years; as in many paintings of this period, the blue has risen to the surface, making the general tone darker than the artist intended.

Most Dutch genre paintings have something anecdotal about them, but Vermeer is always quiet and detached. This becomes apparent if we compare him with Pieter de Hooch, who resembled him in many ways but never quite rose to his level.

This picture was bought for the Dresden Gallery by de Brais, the Secretary of the Legation of Saxony in Paris, in 1742.

JAN VERMEER VAN DELFT (1632–1675)

THE PROCURESS   Canvas

Gallery No. 1335   Height 143 cm. (56$^1/_4$")

Width 130 cm. (51$^1/_8$")

Little is known about Vermeer's life except the years in which he was born, married and died, a few particulars of his activity as a member of the Guild of St Luke at Delft, and some information about various financial trans-actions in which he was for the most part unlucky.

He was a reticent man, and he kept no diaries and wrote no letters which might satisfy our curiosity. When he died, at the age of forty-three, he left debts, a widow with eleven children, and a comparatively small number of pictures, which were forgotten for a long time but are now among the greatest treasures of the world's art.

The pictures are as secretive as the man who painted them. A kind of stillness pervades them all. This is the more curious because his generation was passionate, lively, often blunt, and given to gossip. So there has always been a temptation to try to interpret Vermeer's works, to read into them some message. That saturnine musician in this picture, is he, as has been assumed, a portrait of the artist, then twenty-three years old? And the girl with the bright yellow bodice–is she his wife?

The painter in the picture of the artist's studio, now in Vienna, (believed to represent Vermeer) is dressed exactly like this Dresden musician, but we have only a back view of him, so no definite identification is possible.

The pretty wench appears in several pictures, so it is reasonable to suppose that she was Vermeer's wife, whom he may well have used as a model on several occasions, as painters were in the habit of doing. But is it likely that he would put his own family into a brothel scene?

No sooner do we think that veils are stirring, that hidden secrets are coming to light, than the darkness closes in again, the silence returns. All we can see is a wonderful harmony of colours, a still-life picture of three hands, close together but not touching, a wine-jug, a glass with the play of light upon it, and a thick carpet which seems to act as a barrier between the picture and the spectator.

The work is signed and bears the date 1656. It came from the Wallen-stein collection at Dux, in 1741.

232

CASPAR NETSCHER (1639–1684)

THE LETTER-WRITER Panel

Gallery No. 1346 Height 27 cm. (10⁵/₈")

Width 18.5 cm. (7¹/₄")

An enchanting picture!

The young man has paused in the middle of his letter and sits, chin in hand, gazing into space. We feel sure he is writing a love letter. He is so lost in thought that his right hand, holding the quill pen, has strayed from the sheet of paper to the handsome tablecloth.

The pewter writing set, with sandbox and inkpot on a tray, forms a small still-life of its own.

Vermeer would have left the wall at the back quite plain, contenting himself with the delicate play of light over the bare surface. But to do that successfully would demand a mastery to which Netscher never attained even in his best work. So he prefers to enliven the wall with a map.

It is doubtful whether the artist ever surpassed the delightful intimacy of this picture. Netscher was a pupil of Gerard Ter Borch, several of whose paintings he copied. It was from Ter Borch that he learnt to depict the lustre of silk and satin with such perfection. His middle period was the best. As time went on his colours lost their warmth, to the detriment of the whole composition.

This little picture is signed, and dated 1665. There is a preliminary drawing for it in the British Museum. The first reference to it at Dresden occurs in the inventory for 1722.

234

PIETER VAN SLINGELANDT (1640–1691)
OLD WOMAN PASSING A HEN TO A YOUNG WOMAN
THROUGH THE WINDOW   Panel
Gallery No. 1762   Height 35.5 cm. (13$^7/_8$")
                                              Width 28 cm. (11")

A young woman sits at her lace-making by the open window through
which an old woman is handing her a fowl. A lapdog, its front paws braced
against the floor, is looking up excitedly.

The artist evidently enjoys telling a story, which he decks out with
lavish detail.

Vermeer's interiors are so plain as to appear almost bare by comparison;
he has other and more significant ways of filling his pictures with life.
His rooms and people are self-sufficient; he never uses a window, for
instance, as Slingelandt does here, to make a link between indoors and
outdoors, between the security of home and the wide world of town and
country outside.

Slingelandt carries the miniaturist technique he learnt from his master,
Gerard Dou, almost to the point of bravura. His surface is porcelain-smooth.
Dresden is almost unrivalled among European galleries for the opportunities
it offers of studying and admiring a style of painting and type of subject
which were at one time highly prized.

This little work is signed, and dated 1672 or '73. It first appears in the
inventory for 1722.

236

GERRIT ADRIAENSZ BERCKHEYDE (1638–1698)
STREET IN HAARLEM   Panel
Gallery No. 1523 A   Height 43 cm. (16^7/$_8$″)
                                              Width 39 cm. (15^3/$_8$″)

City scenes made an early appearance in the graphic arts. They were established subjects for drawing and engraving by the end of the fifteenth century – though in the majority of cases, it is true, for strictly topographic purposes. In painting we find them considerably earlier, but only in the subordinate role of background for portraits or for episodes in the lives of the saints.

The credit for introducing this type of painting on a large scale, in its own right, is due to the Dutch artists of the seventeenth century. Painters, with an alert, dispassionate eye for the charms of the factual, wandered all over the towns and set down panoramic views of them, made records of the most remarkable single buildings they passed in streets and squares, and depicted the rooms inside the houses.

This led to the development of a special branch of painting, associated with the names of Jan van der Heyde, Steenwijck, Emmanuel de Witte and Berckheyde.

In this picture of a street at Haarlem, the theme is extremely simple – a street leading to the Grote Kerk, which fills in the background with its compact bulk. The rays of the sun fall obliquely on the stepped, red-brick gables of the houses, while the clean, paved street with the white line down the middle already lies in shadow. The scene is enlivened by a few scattered figures – a horseman greeting a woman in passing, several people on foot and two greyhounds.

The artist has not very much to say, and concentrates on describing the architecture.

This picture came to Dresden in 1912 from the Weber collection at Hamburg.

238

MEINDERT HOBBEMA (1638–1709)

THE WATER MILL

Gallery No. 1664 A

Panel

Height 59.5 cm. (23³/₈″)

Width 84.5 cm. (33¹/₄″)

Hobbema belongs to the second generation of Dutch landscape painting and is its last great exponent. His master was Jacob van Ruisdael, and he comes close to that great philosopher of painting in many of his works, though never equalling him in depth and power of imagination.

Hobbema's landscapes often seem rather cramped, limited in scope, and he tends to linger over finely-detailed studies of clumps of trees and undergrowth. Only once did he succeed in giving an almost monumental spaciousness to a scene from nature. The work in question, *The Avenue, Middelharnis,* was destined to be his most famous picture; it is now in the National Gallery, London.

Hobbema's painting demonstrates how a branch of art which prompted certain innovators – men of genius – to some magnificent works, could degenerate into a form of specialization for knowledgeable amateurs.

His landscapes often repeat a time-honoured theme which reappears yet again in this Dresden picture of the watermill. There is a melancholy air about the farm and the mill on the quiet stretch of water, hidden under ancient, shady trees. Human life, too, seems calm, secure, remote from city bustle. The few small figures that people the scene are, as it were, swallowed up by the landscape. One can understand that nineteenth-century artists found these works particularly attractive.

This picture was bought for the Dresden Gallery in 1899, at the sale of the Schubart collection at Munich.

240

AERT DE GELDER (1645–1727)
THE HALBERDIER   Canvas
Gallery No. 1792   Height 82.5 cm. (32¹/₄″)
                                                       Width 70.5 cm. (27³/₄″)

Aert de Gelder lived at a time when the finest period of Dutch painting
was already over. Imagination and inventiveness, mastery of execution and
nobility of aim were steadily declining into petty genre work and extreme
technical virtuosity. With the arrival of Rococo, the artistic centre of
gravity had begun to shift to France.

This makes it all the more extraordinary that Aert de Gelder should
have been able to carry the tradition of the first half of the seventeenth
century any further. He was Rembrandt's last important pupil, and remained faithful to him at a time when the ageing master had been deserted
by everyone else. The pupil came so close to emulating his great model
that a number of pictures now recognized as the work of de Gelder were
once attributed to Rembrandt.

This *Halberdier* is half-way between portrait and genre painting. The
manner in which the head emerges out of the dark background and catches
the light is typical of the school of Rembrandt.

There is a sturdy, self-reliant air about this armed figure, whose headgear
assumes the firm lines of a helmet. But his face inspires confidence, he
seems to be trying to meet the eyes of the man he is confronting. His
features are soft and rounded, forming a curious contrast to the sharp tip
of the metal halberd.

The King of Saxony bought this picture himself at the Easter Fair at
Leipzig in 1727.

JOSÉ DE RIBERA (1591–1652)
ST AGNES   Canvas
Gallery No. 683   Height 202 cm. (79$^1/_2$")
                                            Width 152 cm. (59$^7/_8$")

St Agnes belonged to one of the leading families of Rome and gave her life for the Christian faith during one of the great persecutions. She lies buried on the Via Nomentana; the tombstone bears the inscription 'Agne sanctissima'. A basilica was erected to her memory as early as the fourth century, by the Emperor Constantine.

The story of her martyrdom has been woven by various ecclesiastical authors into a kind of romance. Ambrose gives some touching particulars. He says that at the time of her execution she was still so small and slight that the fetters they tried to put on her were all too loose and fell off of their own accord.

Pope Damasus writes that when she was stripped naked in order to shame her, her hair grew immediately and abundantly to form a cloak around her.

It is this passage of the legend that Ribera has elected to depict. Agnes has fallen on her knees. Thick hair is falling over her shoulders, right to the ground. An angel has appeared and wrapped her in a white cloth, which she holds in place with her arm as she kneels in prayer. A golden light shines round her.

The picture is signed in full, 'Jusepe de Ribera español. F', and dated 1641. In other words it was painted at a time when the artist had already been living in Naples for twenty-five years. But as the postscript to his signature shows, he had not renounced his Spanish nationality, and he was known in Italy as 'il Spagnoletto'.

There is an air of sombre fanaticism about much of Ribera's work, an impression to which his abrupt transitions from dark to bright patches contribute. That is the Spanish element in his art. But this St Agnes is different, in that it has an appealing quality of homeliness about it. The girl's face shows so much individuality that one is tempted to believe the legend that the artist's own daughter sat for him when it was painted.

The picture came to the Dresden Gallery in 1754 through Count de Bene de Masseran, Spanish Ambassador to the Court of Saxony.

244

FRANCISCO DE ZURBARÁN (1598–1664)
PAPAL ELECTION THROUGH THE INTERVENTION
OF ST BONAVENTURA

Gallery No. 696

Canvas

Height 239 cm. (94^1/$_2$")
Width 222 cm. (87^3/$_8$")

The modern movement in literature includes some writers who succeed in describing commonplace events in a sober, matter-of-fact style which yet discloses a second, underlying reality of which the reader cannot fail to become aware. It is as though a new, fantastic quality were suddenly imparted to the familiar elements of daily life, without modifying their intrinsic character.

Looking closely at Zurbarán's picture of St Bonaventura, one seems to perceive a distant echo of that manner of writing. On the surface, everything looks familiar. The cloth covering the table beside which the Saint kneels in prayer is so realistically painted that we feel we could pick it up. The garland round the silver dish is expertly rendered, it is nothing more nor less than an example of polished technique. As for Bonaventura himself, we feel we have met him somewhere before. His plain Franciscan cowl is draped in folds thrown into relief by the light. The room is plain, too, but its contents are reproduced with unostentatious precision down to the smallest detail.

This sparely-furnished room is suddenly flooded with supernatural light. An angel appears and tells the praying man who is to be elected as the new Pope. He is Cardinal Visconti, of Piacenza, who came to the papal throne as Gregory X. It might be supposed that this invasion from above would make some radical change in the setting. But nothing is changed. Only the silence seems a little more oppressive.

The colour-scheme, like the composition, makes use of a few sharp contrasts – grey and yellow, dominated by the fiery red of the tablecloth, which is echoed in the robes of the waiting Cardinals in the background.

The picture came to the Dresden Gallery from the collection of Louis-Philippe in London, in 1853.

246

EL GRECO (1541–1614)
CHRIST HEALING THE BLIND MAN   Panel
Gallery No. 276   Height 65.5 cm. (25³/₄″)
Width 84 cm. (33¹/₈″)

The Bible speaks of Christ restoring sight to the blind on several occasions. El Greco seems to have chosen the episode related in the Gospel according to St Mark (Chap. 8, 22–26), in which Christ is described as taking the blind man by the hand, leading him outside the village, and healing him by the laying on of hands.

El Greco places his chief group, including Christ, to the left of his composition. To the right and towards the centre are the disciples and a few other people, in excited conversation. It seems curious that the artist should have left the middle of the picture completely empty – a vacuum that exerts a certain force of attraction. This effect is strengthened by the steep downward-sloping lines of the perspective.

Clouds are driving across the sky, their restless movement echoing the gesticulation of the people below. Even the group round Christ seems to vibrate with inner tension.

The colour, on the contrary, is cold and unemotional – a combination of steel-blue, olive-green, yellowish grey and purple.

The artist, whose real name was Domenico Theotokopolous, was born in Candia in Crete. He went to Venice, where he became a pupil of Titian, and was strongly influenced by him, as well as by Tintoretto and the Bassani.

He visited Rome in 1570, leaving that city for Toledo in Spain, where he is recorded to have obtained citizenship by 1577.

He did not leave Toledo again – apart from visits to Madrid – dying there in the year 1641.

248

This work dates from his early Venetian period. Several replicas have survived. A signed variant is now in the gallery at Parma.

The Dresden version was bought for the Gallery by Rossi at Venice in 1741.

DIEGO VELÁSQUEZ (1599–1660)
PORTRAIT OF A MAN
Gallery No. 697

Canvas
Height 108 cm. (42¹/₂")
Width 89 cm. (35")

The model for this portrait is believed to be Juan Mateos, Grand Master of the Royal Hunt. Hunting played a great part in Spanish court life during the seventeenth century; Philip IV himself had a passion for it. Alfonso Martínez de Espinar says in his *Arte de Ballestería y Monetría* (1644) that by the age of thirty-nine the King had already killed 400 wolves, 600 bucks and 150 wild boars—an unusually high total. In these circumstances the office of Grand Master of the Hunt can have been no sinecure. It was a position of trust, and the holder was also responsible for other confidential tasks that arose from time to time.

Velásquez' portrait shows a man of advanced age, already somewhat corpulent. The sombre effect of his black patterned coat with its black sash is lightened somewhat by narrow white collar. The grey head with the pointed beard is impressive; one feels that this man is really fitted for high office. His expression and bearing inspire respect. The artist can therefore dispense with the adjuncts upon which so many Baroque painters relied to render the rank and status of their models convincing. Velásquez relies entirely on facial expression. Only Juan Mateos' hand, resting on the hilt of his dagger, gives any outward hint of his position.

However cool and aloof their attitude, Velásquez' sitters are always natural and full of life. They do not carry us away, but they radiate energy and strength. They keep their distance, but they are never remote. Velásquez allows a modicum of dignity and humanity even to the poorest and most lowly courtier.

This portrait of the Master of the Hunt is unfinished; the hands are not painted with realistic exactitude. This sketchy treatment seems to foreshadow Manet. But the effect is not intentional. It is simply that we are shown here, more clearly than usual—for in a finished painting it is hidden beneath the surface—a means of artistic creation which was to be revived and perfected by the Impressionists in the nineteenth century.

This picture was originally in the ducal gallery at Modena, where it was entered as a Rubens 'with the sketched-in hands'. It came from there to Dresden in 1746.

250

BARTOLOMÉ ESTEBAN MURILLO (1618–1682)

ST RODRIGUEZ   Canvas
Gallery No. 704   Height 205 cm. (80³/₄")
                                          Width 123 cm. (48³/₈")

The Saint is standing beside a stone balustrade. He wears an alb and a magnificently embroidered chasuble. We can see the wound of martyrdom in his throat. He is gazing up in rapture at the cloudy sky, his arms slightly outstretched as though to receive a blessing from above. A cherub is swooping down to crown him with a wreath of flowers.

Murillo's art has a quality of simple, heartfelt piety, devoid of any ascetic or intellectual element. With this goes an amiable, courteous treatment of the model and a style of composition that flows in gentle lines. The colour is deep and has a quality of restrained sensuousness. Shafts of light play over his scenes, softening all the contours with faint shadows. Harsh facts, such as any reference to a martyr's death, are delicately passed over or merely hinted at.

Throughout his life, Murillo drew upon the rich reserves of the Spanish folk tradition. This gave his art a 'living' quality which has never lost its freshness. The mention of his name at once brings to mind the cheerful little ragamuffins, the beggars and fruiteaters, he portrayed so vividly. Even his sweet-faced Madonnas, with their big, dark eyes, are girls from among the people who never disavow their origin.

Murillo was a native of Seville, in southern Spain, where Zurbarán, twenty years his senior, also lived; but his character had nothing in common with that brooding nature.

This picture of St Rodriguez belongs to Murillo's middle period. It came to Dresden in 1853 from the Louis-Philippe collection in London.

252

VALENTIN DE BOULOGNE (1591–1634)

THE CARD SHARPER

Gallery No. 408

Canvas

Height 94.5 cm. (37^1/$_4$")
Width 137 cm. (53^7/$_8$")

This picture was long attributed to Caravaggio – until, in 1906, it was found to bear the signature of Valentin de Boulogne. Indeed, it reveals many of the characteristics of the great Roman painter, who was the chief influence in Valentin's development.

Caravaggio was a rash, turbulent man, addicted to brawling, but of tremendous charm; he came to a tragic end at the early age of thirty-six. Even when dealing with religious subjects, Caravaggio's style is extremely objective and often marked by an almost brutal realism. All his figures are modelled in the round; they emerge from a background of strongly contrasted light and shade. There is often something languid about his colours. Yet over all this, even when it seems most banal, there lies what has been well described as a *tristezza mortale,* a fatalism, which gives a melancholy nobility to Caravaggio's work.

Not one of his many imitators and admirers rose to the same level. Manfredi, Vouet, even Valentin himself merely copied his technique and never advanced beyond the palpably realistic. This picture of *The Card Sharper* is nevertheless among the most successful works of the whole movement – perhaps because it promises no more than it can achieve, and is thus able to come as near as possible to perfection within its own limits.

Two young soldiers sit at a rough wooden table in some Roman guardroom (the artist gives no more precise information than this). One man is hiding an extra card behind his back while a third fellow looks over his opponent's shoulder and makes signs to the cheat. A harsh light falls on a patch of red, a patch of yellow, and glints metallically from weapons and coins.

The handsome, careless faces seem familiar; these are the typical *ragazzi* introduced into art by Caravaggio and taken over by Honthorst, Terbrugghen, Michael Sweerts and – in his youth – Velásquez.

This picture came to Dresden in 1749 from the Imperial Gallery at Prague.

254

NICOLAS POUSSIN (1594–1665)

PAN AND SYRINX   Canvas

Gallery No. 718   Height 106 cm. (41^3/$_4$″)

                                              Width 82 cm. (32^1/$_4$″)

It is certainly no mere coincidence that the two greatest French painters of the seventeenth century should both have elected to live in Rome. Claude Lorrain, the landscape painter, spent his whole time there from early childhood; Nicolas Poussin settled there in 1624 and remained, with one two-year interval, for the rest of his life. In those days Rome was a centre of attraction not only for artists from all over Italy, such as Bernini, Caravaggio, the Carracci, Domenichino and Guercino, but for Germans and Dutch, including, among many others, Elsheimer, Rubens, Van Dyck, Paulus Bril, Sweerts and Pieter van Laer, and their meetings led to much fruitful give and take of ideas.

These men had various reasons for going to Rome. But what drew the two French painters there and held them all their lives was an instinctive longing for grace, proportion and form – in short, for the classical element which is latent in all French art and which, at a period when Baroque was at its most ornate, could nowhere find such profound and complete expression as at the very fountain-head of classical antiquity.

It is evident that Poussin thereby received a considerable stimulus from contemporaries with whom he had affinities and from painters belonging to the recent past, such as Domenichino, Annibale Carracci, Titian and Raphael.

Both the style and the content of the art of antiquity interested him – the poems of Ovid, for instance, provided an inexhaustible fund of themes. It is from the First Book of *Metamorphoses* that the episode of Pan and Syrinx derives.

We see Pan, the goat-footed god of mountains and flocks, driven by Cupid, who brandishes a torch, in pursuit of the nymph Syrinx, whom Ladon, the river-god, has drawn protectively into his arms. The reed into which the god is about to transform the fugitive is already growing in the background of the picture.

The scene is like a bas-relief, with the vigorously modelled figures all on one plane. The general effect is gay and relaxed; only on closer inspection do we realize how systematically the composition is built up.

This picture was acquired for Dresden from the Dubreuil collection in Paris, through de Brais, in 1742.

256

NICOLAS POUSSIN (1594–1665)
NARCISSUS AND ECHO
Gallery No. 722

Canvas
Height 72 cm. ($28^3/8''$)
Width 96.5 cm. (38")

In his *Kingdom of Flora* (see page 26) Poussin did not always follow Ovid punctiliously. For instance he shows the nymph Echo in that picture as a charming young girl, who sits watching Narcissus as he dies – whereas according to the poet, grief over her spurned love had turned her to stone long before Nemesis punished the youth for his hard-heartedness by condemning him to languish to death in futile adoration of his reflection. The story of Echo and Narcissus as Ovid relates it had already been handled by Poussin in the early work shown here, which was probably painted soon after his arrival in Rome.

The deluded youth lies beside a woodland pool, fascinated by his own image and heedless of the two water-nymphs who sit watching him. Echo's form is outlined in a block of stone. Only her voice is still alive; she repeats the lovesick ninny's every sigh, and this merely deepens his madness.

In the end he sighed himself to death. Those who came to bury him found no corpse, only 'a saffron-coloured flower with a ring of white petals round its centre' – the narcissus.

The mythical presentation of life and death as elements of the great processes of Nature, is the subject thoughtfully treated here by Poussin. It was a theme to which he often returned.

In this early picture the composition is rather academic, it falls into the pattern of a right-angled triangle. The artist has not yet achieved the mastery of modelling, drawing and colour which makes his later work so fascinating. The red pigment used as a base has worked through and makes the whole colour-scheme heavier than was originally intended. The bright ice-blue of which Poussin was so fond, and which features in so many of his paintings, is already seen here in the cloak of the seated nymph.

This picture was bought for the Dresden Gallery through Le Plat in Paris, in 1725.

258

NICOLAS POUSSIN (1594–1665)

THE KINGDOM OF FLORA   Canvas

Gallery No. 719   Height 131 cm. (51⅝″)
                                                    Width 181 cm. (71¼″)

Flora is sweetly smiling as she dances round, scattering blossoms. All the
mythological figures who were destined to be turned into flowers at their
death are gathered around her – Narcissus with the nymph Echo, the wreath-
crowned Crocus towards whom the nymph Smilax is gliding (she became
a wind); behind them stands Adonis, vigorously beautiful, pointing to the
death-wound on his thigh where the boar's tusk pierced him; and finally the
enchanting Hyacinth, who was accidentally killed by Apollo with an
unlucky throw when they were competing at quoits. On the other side of the
painting the nymph Klytiax is gazing up into the firmament across which
the radiant Phoebus, her faithless lover, is driving the chariot of the Sun,
while the hero Ajax falls heavily on his sword, as the pink which is to drink
his blood springs out of the ground. Narcissus, Crocus and Hyacinth already
bear the names of the flowers in which they are to be immortalized. Klytiax
was changed into the heliotrope, Adonis into the anemone, and Echo into
a stone.

'Transformation' is common to all the figures depicted here. They gather
cheerfully to meet their death, with Cupids frolicking round them, in the
shadow of a statue of Priapus, beside a fountain with water flowing over its
stone brim. The scene is closed in by a light, graceful pergola with plants
growing delicately over it.

The artist has handled the difficult problem of composition with extraordinary ease and grace. The figures are placed, individually or in groups,
along the horizontal, vertical or diagonal lines of the picture, and all
combine to form a gentle ellipse. The whole work has been carefully planned
and is expressed in precise, almost phonetically simplified terms. It reminds
us of Corneille's powerful declamatory style. It is a wonder that this
conscious, deliberate mastery can have been applied without destroying the
fragile magic on which the work of art depends for its life.

Is it the mysterious light, softening all angles and bringing out the pure,
radiant colours, which creates the spell? Is it the experience of a mature
artist, effortlessly expressed in symbols which are easy to interpret? It is one
thing to ask such questions, another thing to answer them. The ultimate
mysteries of great art are a subject for contemplation, not for analysis.

The *Kingdom of Flora* first appears in the inventory for 1722, with no
particulars of how it was acquired.

260

CLAUDE LORRAIN (1600–1682)

LANDSCAPE WITH THE REST ON THE FLIGHT INTO EGYPT　　　　　Canvas

Gallery No. 730　　　　　　　　　　　　　　Height 102 cm. (40$^1/_8$")

　　　　　　　　　　　　　　　　　　　Width 134 cm. (52$^3/_4$")

Claude Gellée (to give him his real name) was a native of Champagne, in Lorraine. He went to Rome in his childhood and remained there all his life, and there he was given the nickname 'Lorrain', by which he later became generally known.

In his work the idealized style of landscape painting, which originated in Rome about 1600, attained its purest and most perfect expression.

As the words 'idealized landscape' suggest, at the root of this lay an invented, artificial arrangement of nature – a cleaned-up version, in its Sunday best, so to speak, where all is harmony and melody; nature as it might sometimes appear in the Roman Campagna on a beautiful evening. Antiquity makes its contribution, with memories of the classical writers, especially Virgil and Ovid, who give such incomparable descriptions of these scenes in their poems.

In most of Claude's works a cluster of shady trees stands to one side of the picture, leaving an unbroken view over a well-watered plain that stretches to the blue distances of the horizon, where it is cut off by a ridge of steep hills. But his art works its magic chiefly through light, which floods the scene with a golden glow and creates a lyrical mood. It is usually cast by the evening sun as it sinks towards the west, throwing long shadows which suggest that it is time to return home.

Thus, the note of farewell is struck almost as soon as the landscape painters embark on their happy theme.

The picture is signed and dated, CLAVDE IVEF ROMA 1647. In the *Liber Veritatis* it appears as No. 110, painted for M. Purasson, of Lyons. Thence it came to Madame de Verrue's collection in Paris and passed into the Nocet collection in 1725. Finally it came into the hands of Graf von Hoym, the Saxon Ambassador to Paris, and was probably acquired from him for the Dresden Gallery. Its first mention there occurs in the inventory for 1754.

262

CLAUDE LORRAINE (1600–1682)

ACIS AND GALATEA   Canvas

Gallery No. 731   Height 100 cm. (39³/₈")

                     Width 135 cm. (53¹/₈")

It would never have occurred to anybody in the seventeenth century, or even in the eighteenth, to paint a landscape with no figures. Nature was regarded as a setting for human beings, whose presence gave it significance. Not until the early nineteenth century did artists discover the completely unpeopled landscape, the charm of nature considered on its own merits.

Claude took his figures from the Bible or, preferably, from classical mythology.

The story of Acis and Galatea, represented in this picture, is told by Ovid in his *Metamorphoses* (XIII, 738–897). Galatea, daughter of Nereus and Doris, was a sea-nymph. Her lover, Acis, was killed out of jealousy by Polyphemus, the Cyclops. The one-eyed giant failed to win the bereaved nymph's affection, and Acis was transformed into a river-god.

Claude's picture is sheer poetry. The lovers are embracing outside a pinkish-mauve tent on the seashore, surrounded by playful Cupids and two billing doves. As a presage of their impending fate, Polyphemus and his flock are shown on a distant spur of cliff, in the rays of the setting sun. So here again the word 'farewell' echoes in counter-point.

The picture is signed CLAUDE GELEE IVEF ROMA 1657. According to the *Liber Veritatis*, the record of his paintings made by Claude, where it bears the number 141, it was painted in 1657 for M. Delagard.

Together with *Liber Veritatis* No. 110, it went in turn to the de Verrue and de Nocet collections.

264

From thence the painting went into the hands of the Saxon Ambassador to Paris, and in all probability was acquired from him by the Dresden Gallery, where it is first mentioned in the inventory for 1754.

265

ANTOINE WATTEAU (1684–1721)

FÊTE CHAMPÊTRE   Canvas
Gallery No. 781   Height 60 cm. (23⅝")
                                                          Width 75 cm. (29½")

Watteau was described by his few intimates as morose, difficult, unsociable and pessimistic. He lacked all confidence in his artistic ability and was always liable, in an attack of exasperated depression, to decide that his current picture was a failure and destroy it.

It was the fate of this undistinguished looking, sickly painter, who chose to struggle on in dire poverty rather than be dependent on wealthy friends and patrons, to live at a time when a brilliant position, charm, good looks and worldly success were the only things that counted.

This makes it all the more amazing, even pathetic, that he should have produced such graceful, enchanting work, in which no hint of his wretched circumstances is allowed to escape–unless it be the faint melancholy that pervades some of his pictures, particularly those of the last years, the period of his greatest maturity.

It is a melancholy that slowly transmutes Watteau's landscapes, the poetic parks in which his *Fêtes Galantes* are set, into autumnal gold, while the word 'farewell' lingers unspoken in the air.

A characteristic restlessness marks the work of this artist, who was to die of tuberculosis at the age of thirty-seven. But though many of his pictures were painted in tremendous haste, they show no sign of fatigue or carelessness. For all their bubble-lightness and spontaneity they are planned to the smallest detail, their form is perfect and their psychology convincing. These are inspired compositions, made in defiance of a subjective and objective experience completely at variance with their spirit.

Some potentially creative personalities may well have been silenced for ever by circumstances such as those which Watteau had to face, coupled with temperament like his. Others, again, set themselves the task of recording their problems in all their harsh reality. Of these, Goya is an outstanding example.

This picture is mentioned for the first time in 1753 in the Guarienti inventory.

266

ANTOINE WATTEAU (1684–1721)
LA FÊTE D'AMOUR   Canvas
Gallery No. 728   Height 61 cm. (24″)
                                             Width 75 cm. (29¹/₂″)

A preliminary study made by Watteau for this picture has been preserved. It
is unique of its kind, for though Watteau was a prolific draughtsman, his
paintings were nearly all spontaneous creations, for which he made no
preparatory sketches or plans. True, he introduced into his works some of
the single figures he used to draw in sanguine and chalk; but however
finished and successful these might be (and the artist thought more highly
of some of them than of his paintings, with which he was never satisfied!),
he used them as a kind of raw material, never regarding them as intellectual
forerunners of the actual pictures in which they appeared.

This is typical of Watteau, in whose creative work two trends were
combined—a streak of realism derived from his Flemish background, and a
completely spiritual element which was his own personal contribution. And
although these trends come out individually, one in his drawings and the
other in his paintings, they nevertheless tend to fuse and in one way or
another inform the artist's entire *œuvre*.

The drawing for *La fête d'amour*, then, is exceptional, because for once
the basic idea of the final painting is expressed completely. Three pairs of
lovers are lying on the grass in the shadow of a statue of Venus, while
another couple steals away, with backward glances. So here again the
'farewell' motif is repeated.

The drawing is light and airy, as though itself seeking to attain to the
indescribable perfection of sublimated colour achieved by the final painting.
Watteau's style is not anecdotic, so descriptions of the content of his pictures
in no way convey the real, individual essence of the work. What is of
importance is their inner balance, their dispassionate attitude, which can
even dispel the underlying pain.

Like the previous picture, this one belongs to Watteau's later period.
It is entered in the Guarienti inventory.

268

MAURICE QUENTIN DE LA TOUR (1704–1788)
PORTRAIT OF MAURICE OF SAXONY, MARSHAL OF FRANCE   Pastel
Gallery No. P. 164   Height 59.5 cm. $(23^3/8'')$
                                                Width 49 cm. $(19^1/4'')$

Maurice of Saxony was a natural son of Augustus the Strong by Countess Aurora von Königsmark; in 1711, when he was fifteen years old, his father legitimized him and gave him the title Count of Saxony.

Before long he left his native land, serving in the French army in 1720. In 1744, after winning many victories for France, he was promoted Marshal, a high distinction. He died at Chambord in 1750, when only fifty-four years of age. A splendid monument to him, in which the classicist spirit is already strongly evidenced, was designed by Pigalle and stands in the church of St Thomas in Strasbourg.

La Tour's portrait shows him as a pleasant-looking man. His dress – a russet jacket trimmed with dark brown fur – looks unassumingly comfortable. Only the white Order of the Eagle on his chest, with its pale blue ribbon, reminds us that he is a soldier. And despite the firm, manly features, the impression created by the softly curling grey hair, the close-fitting dress and the relaxed, meditative pose is more that of a man of letters.

And indeed, the Count's published writings show him to have been an exceptionally intelligent man. His *Rêveries militaires,* which are full of bold ideas, appeared in 1731, and his *Lettres et Mémoires* were collected after his death and published in 1794. Scribe wrote a play about his meeting with the famous actress, Adrienne Lecouvreur.

La Tour was a great portraitist. He possessed the ability to express complex relationships convincingly within the narrow bounds of portraiture. This is one of those mysteries of communication which cannot be explained by reason alone. It is a curious fact that he confined himself almost entirely to pastel. A comparison with the work of Rosalba Carriera shows that everything depends on the quality of the artist. Anyone acquainted only with Carriera's portraits would scarcely believe that the powerful effect achieved by La Tour could be produced by the same medium.

The *Portrait of Maurice of Saxony* first appears in the 1765 catalogue, with no indication of how it was acquired.

270

ITALIAN SCHOOL

Siennese School Madonna and Child

Siennese School Madonna (detail)

*Cosimo **Tura***
St Sebastian

Ercole di Roberti Christ taken Prisoner

Ercole di Roberti Christ taken to Golgatha

Jacopo de Barbari
Christ in Benediction

Botticelli Madonna and Child
with John the Baptist

Lorenzo Costa Madonna reading

273

Francesco Francia The Adoration of the Magi

Lorenzo di Credi
Adoration of the Infant Christ

Palma Vecchio Sleeping Venus

Palma Vecchio Three Sisters

Franciabigio The Story of Bathsheba

Bartolommeo Veneto
Salome with the Head
of John the Baptist

Andrea del Sarto
The Mystic Marriage of St Catherine

Correggio
Madonna with St Sebastian

274

Correggio
Madonna with St George

Correggio Madonna with St Francis

Lorenzo Lotto Madonna and Child
with the Infant St John

Titian Madonna and Child with Four Saints

Titian Titian's daughter, Lavinia

Titian Painter with a Palm-branch

Giulio Romano The Madonna del Catino

Bacchiaccia Archery Practice upon a Dead Man

Garofalo Athene and Poseidon

Parmigianino
Madonna and Child in Glory

Girolamo Mazzola Bedoli
Madonna and Child

Andrea Schiavone The Body of Christ,
supported by an Angel
and Joseph of Arimathea

Veronese
Portrait of Alessandro Contarini

Veronese The Resurrection

276

Veronese Madonna with the Cuccina family

Veronese The Adoration of the Magi

Tintoretto Portrait of a Lady in Mourning

Tintoretto Christ and the Woman taken in Adultery

Tintoretto The Liberation of Arsinoë

Federico Barocci Virgin and Child on the Flight into Egypt

Dossi St George

277

Francesco Albani
Galatea in her Shell Chariot

Domenico Fetti Archimedes

Bernardo Strozzi Rebecca at the Well

Guido Reni Madonna Enthroned
with the Christ-child

Carracci Allegory of Fame

Carracci Madonna and Child
with the Infant John
the Baptist offering a Swallow

Carracci Christ Crowned with Thorns

Carracci Madonna in Glory
with St Matthew

Procaccini The Holy Family

278

Alessandro Turchi Venus and Adonis

Guercino St Veronica

Pietro Negri Nero and the Body of Agrippina

Cerquozzi Looting after Battle

Salvatore Rosa Wooded Landscape
with Three Philosophers

Carlo Dolci St Cecilia
playing the Organ

Mattia Preti The Martyrdom
of St Bartholomew

Carlo Maratti(a)
Madonna bending over the Crib

Luca Giordano St Irene and
the martyred St Sebastian

Bartolommeo Chiari The Adoration of the Kings

Sebastiano Ricci Sacrifice to Vesta

Francesco Trevisani The Rest on the Flight into Egypt

Francesco Solimena The Vision of St Francis

Crespi Baptism

Crespi Consecration of a Priest

280

Alessandro Magnasco
Nuns in the Choir

Carriera A Venetian Procurator

Carriera Portrait of the Dancer,
Barbarina Campani

Piazetta The Sacrifice of Abraham

Rotari Sleeping Girl

Tiepolo
The Vision of St Anne

Bellotto The Marketplace at Pirna

Bellotto New Marketplace at Dresden,
seen from the Moritzstrasse

281

GERMAN SCHOOL

School of Dürer
Christ nailed to the Cross

School of Dürer
The Circumcision

Master of the 'Embroidered Leaves'
St Christopher

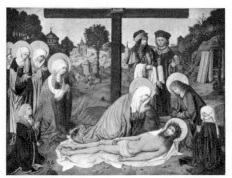

Master of the Hausbuch Lamentation over the Dead Christ

Hans Maler
Portrait of Joachim Rehle

Jorg Breu the Elder
The St Ursula Altarpiece

Lucas Cranach
Christ on the Mount of Olives

Lucas Cranach
St Catherine

Lucas Cranach
St Barbara

282

Lucas Cranach The Garden of Eden   *Lucas Cranach* Adam   *Lucas Cranach* Eve

Georg Pencz
Adoration of the
Kings (Detail)

Lucas Cranach the Younger
Hercules and the Pigmies

Josef Heintz The Rape of Proserpina

Josef Heintz Ecce Homo   *Adam Elsheimer* Jupiter and Mercury in the House
of Philemon and Baucis

283

Rottenhammer
The Rest on the Flight into Egypt

Knüpfer The Painter and his Family

Johann Anton Eismann Ruins by a River

Karl Skreta St Gregory

Schönfeldt
Entertainment at the Spinet

Christoph Paudiss
Portrait of a Young Man

Abraham Mignon Vase of Flowers

284

Johann Heiss The Israelites leaving Egypt

Philipp Peter Roos Shepherd and his Flock

Faistenberger Mountain Landscape with Nymphs

Franz de Paula Ferg Fair in front of a Castle

Wenzel Lorenz Reiner Roman Cattlemarket

Johann Alexander Thiele The Elbe in Frost and Fog

Ismael Mengs Self-portrait

Johann Georg Platzer Croesus and Solon

Anton Kern The Massacre of the Innocents

Christian Wilhelm Dietrich The Resurrection of Lazarus

Christian Seybold Boy with a Flute

Anton Raphael Mengs
The Artist's Father, Ismael Mengs

Anton Raphael Mengs
Cupid sharpening his Arrow

286

Oeser The Artist's Sons　　*Hackert* Civita Castellana　　*Anton Graff* Youthful Self-portrait

Angelica Kauffmann Ariadne forsaken　　*Fuseli* Hero, Ursula and Beatrice　　*Daniel Caffe*
Portrait of Caroline Riquet

Christian Leberecht Vogel The Artist's Sons　　*Johann Christian Klengel* Arcadian Landscape

287

Herri met de Bles Monkeys stealing from a Peddler

Herri met de Bles John the Baptist preaching

Joachim Buekelaer
The Four Evangelists

Maerten van Valckenborch The Tower of Babel

Gillis van Coninxloo The Judgement of Midas

Paul Bril Landscape with Roman Ruins

'Velvet' Brueghel Landscape with the Call
of the Apostles Peter and Andrew

'Velvet' Brueghel
Houses at the Waterside, behind Trees

'Velvet' Brueghel Woodcutters by a River

'Velvet' Brueghel Road on a Wooded Hill

Joos de Momper Mountain Landscape

Joos de Momper The Town in the Valley

Joos de Momper
Mountain Landscape with a Water Mill

David Vinckeboons Kermesse beneath the Trees

Rubens Mercury and Argus

Rubens St Francis of Paula implored for help
from the Sick of the Plague

289

Rubens Druken Hercules

Rubens Quos Ego

Rubens Portrait of a Woman with Braided Hair

Rubens The Judgement of Paris

Rubens Leda and the Swan

Rubens Hero and Leander

Hendrick van Steenwijck Interior of a Gothic Church

Jan Wildens Winter Landscape with Huntsman

290

Adriaen Brouwer Peasants fighting
during a Game of Dice

Adriaen Brouwer
Unpleasant Parental Duties

Nicolas Regnier St Sebastian

Van Dyck Portrait of a Man
drawing on his Gloves

Van Dyck Portrait of a Lady
with a Golden Chain

Van Dyck St Jerome

Lucas van Uden Landscape with a Wedding Procession

Jordaens Diogenes with his Lantern

291

Jordaens The Family of Christ
at the Sepulchre

Jordaens Ariadne and Bacchus

Jan Fijt A Boy and a Dwarf with a big Dog

Peter Gysels Rocky River Valley with a Village,
a Church and a Windmill

Teniers The Dentist

Teniers The Temptation of St Anthony

Teniers The Liberation of St Peter

Teniers The Bleaching-ground

292

DUTCH SCHOOL

Dutch School Christ taken Prisoner

Dutch School Portrait of Man
with Three Arrows

Cornelis Engelbrechtsen
The Temptation of St Anthony

Joos van Cleve The Deposition

Antonio Moro
Portrait of a Man

Marinus van Reymerswaele
The Money Changer and his Wife

Jan van Scorel David and Goliath

293

Hans Bol Village Fair

Hans Bol Meleagar and Atalanta

Hans Bol Moses at the Well

Roeland Savery Ruined Tower on the Vogelweiher

Hendrick Gerritsz Pot
Portrait of a Man

Johann Lis The Penitent Magdalene

Hendrick Avercamp Games on the Ice

294

Gerhard van Honthorst The Dentist

Pieter Claesz Still-life

Cornelis van Poelenburgh Parnassus

Jan van Goyen A Well near Cottages

Salomon Koninck The Astronomer

Josef de Bray Still-life

Thomas de Keyser Two Horsemen

Jan Vermeer van Haarlem
View of Sandhills on the Dutch Plain

Salomon Jacobsz van Ruysdael
Wooded River Bank

Rembrandt
Self-portrait with Sketchbook

Rembrandt
Portrait of Willem Burchgraeff

Rembrandt Old Man with a Beard

Rembrandt Manoah's Offering

Rembrandt Rembrandt's wife,
Saskia van Uijlenburgh, as a young girl

296

Aert van der Neer Canal in a Village

Jan Asselijn Young Herdsman with Cattle at the Stream

Jan Davidsz. de Heem Still-life with Bird's Nest

Govert Flinck Portrait of Rembrandt(?)

Bartholomaus van der Helst The Wife of the Burgomaster

Hendrick Maertansz Sorgh Fish-wife of Rotterdam

Wouwerman Stag-hunt by a River

Wouwerman The Hangman's House

297

Wouwerman Cavalry Battle in front of a Burning Windmill

Gerard Dou Still-life

Gerard Dou Rembrandt's Mother

Gerard Dou Violin-player at the Window

Gerard Dou The Dentist

Gerard Dou The Painter in his Studio

Herman Saftleven the Younger View of Utrecht

Paulus Potter Resting Herd

298

Gebrandt van den Eeckhout Jacob's Dream   *Allaert van Everdingen* Stag Hunt in a Mountain Lake

Gerard ter Borch
Officer reading a Letter

Adriaen van Ostade
Peasants at an Inn Table

Adriaen van Ostade
Two Peasants smoking

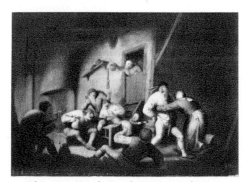 

Adriaen van Ostade Rowdy Peasants in the Inn   *Ferdinand Bol* The Rest on the Flight into Egypt

Claes Berchem Reception of the Moorish Envoy

Philips de Koninck Landscape

Gabriel Metsu The Lace-maker

Gabriel Metsu
Young Woman selling Poultry

Gabriel Metsu The Poultry-vendor

Jan Steen The Marriage at Cana

Jacob van Ruisdael The Monastery

300

Jacob van Ruisdael The Hunt

Adriaen van de Velde Cattle Grazing

Job Berckheyde Interior of the Great Church at Haarlem

Melchior d'Hondecoeter Concert of Birds

Jacob Ochtervelt The Gallant

Frans van Mieris The Lover's Message

Cornelis de Heem Still-life with Oysters

301

Caspar Netscher Lady singing

Berckheyde View of the Dam at Amsterdam
and the Town Hall

Ludolf Backhuysen Battle at Sea

Jan Griffier A Fair in a River Valley

Aert de Gelder The Document

Aert de Gelder The Mocking of Christ

Jan van der Heyden The Old Palace in Brussels

302

SPANISH SCHOOL

Luis de Morales The Man of Sorrows

Ribera Diogenes with his Lantern

Velásquez Portrait of an Old Man

Valdés Leal St Vasco of Portugal

Bartolomé Esteban Murillo Madonna and Child

303

FRENCH SCHOOL

Bartholomaus Dietterlin
Wooded Landscape with Diana and Actaeon

Nicolas Poussin Sleeping Venus

Nicolas Poussin Moses in the Bullrushes

Nicolas Poussin Adoration of the Magi

Largillière Portrait of
Chamberlain de Montargu

Louis de Silvestre
Portrait of General Jan de Bodt

Antoine Pesne
Girl with Pigeons

Liotard Maurice of Saxony

Quentin de La Tour
Marie-Josephe, Dauphine of France

LIST OF ILLUSTRATIONS

Page numbers in bold type refer to colour plates

305

306

308

309

310

312

313

314

316

318

INDEX OF NAMES

Page numbers in italics refer to the notes on the colour plates